Privilege
Revealed

Critical America

General Editors: RICHARD DELGADO and JEAN STEFANCIC

White by Law:
The Legal Construction of Race
Ian F. Haney López

Cultivating Intelligence:
Power, Law, and the Politics of Teaching
Louise Harmon and Deborah W. Post

Privilege Revealed:
How Invisible Preference Undermines America
Stephanie M. Wildman
with contributions by Margalynne Armstrong,
Adrienne D. Davis, and Trina Grillo

Privilege Revealed

How Invisible Preference Undermines America

Stephanie M. Wildman
with contributions by
Margalynne Armstrong,
Adrienne D. Davis, and Trina Grillo

NEW YORK UNIVERSITY PRESS
New York and London

NEW YORK UNIVERSITY PRESS

New York and London

Library of Congress Cataloging-in-Publication Data

Wildman, Stephanie M., 1949–
Privilege revealed: how invisible preference undermines America /
Stephanie M. Wildman with Margalynne Armstrong ... [et al.].
p. cm. — (Critical America)
Includes bibliographical references and index.
Contents: Making systems of privilege visible—Privilege in the
workplace—Privilege in residential housing—Privilege and the
media—Obscuring the importance of race—Comparisons between
racism and sexism (or other -isms)—The dream of diversity and the
cycle of exclusion—The quest for justice—Teaching and learning
toward transformation—Concluding thoughts on noticing privilege.
1. Power (Social sciences)—United States. 2. Equality—United
States. I. Title. II. Series.
HN90.P6W56 1996
303.3—dc20   96-4483
                                             CIP

Koosh ball is a registered trademark of Oddzon Products, Inc., Campbell, CA.

Wite-Out is a registered trademark of Wite-Out Products, Inc., Beltsville, MD.

New York University Press books are printed on acid-free paper,
and their binding materials are chosen for strength and durability.

Manufactured in the United States of America

10 9 8 7 6 5 4 3 2 1

For

Becky Wildman-Tobriner
Ben Wildman-Tobriner
Luisa Grillo-Chope
Jeffrey Grillo
Rebecca Buckner Pierce
and the future of all the children.

In memory of Lena Sokol

Contents

Acknowledgments

Thank you first and foremost to Richard Delgado and Jean Stefancic, series editors of Critical America, without whose support this book would not have come to exist. I am grateful to the community of scholars involved in critical race theory, critical legal studies, and feminist critical theory, whose work has created a community that makes the expression of these ideas possible. Thanks also to my students and faculty colleagues at Santa Clara Law School, Hastings College of the Law, Stanford Law School, and the University of San Francisco School of Law, where I have taught about these issues.

I would like to recognize my intellectual debt to two colleagues, Adrienne Davis and Trina Grillo, both professors of law and both women of color. The three of us worked together for almost two years, writing several working papers examining systems of privilege. I know that I am able to see more now, because of my friendship with them. More recently, I have benefited greatly from time spent with Margalynne Armstrong, another African American law professor.

I also owe particular thanks to Trina, Adrienne, and Margalynne, along with Edith Wildman, Herman Wildman, Emily Goldman, Dr. Russell Leong, Carole Shauffer, and Catharine Wells, for patiently reading drafts of this manuscript. Gloria Gonzàlez and the support staff at Santa Clara Law School have my appreciation for superlative assistance in preparing the manuscript. As always, Lee Ryan and Marian Shostrom provided professional and caring research support. NYU Press made the final stages a writer's dream.

Finally, thanks and love to Michael Tobriner, Becky Wildman-Tobriner, and Ben Wildman-Tobriner, because it is not always easy to live with someone who is writing a book.

STEPHANIE M. WILDMAN

Stephanie M. Wildman

A Note about Systems of Privilege

Many contemporary theorists have emphasized the social construction of race. The idea of race exists because people give it particular meaning, a meaning that changes with time, place, and circumstances. But one constant remains—the privileging of whiteness through different devices, social patterns, and even laws. This racial positioning is maintained in part through an unwritten rule that it cannot be discussed. In fact, the corollary rule mandates that we talk about the societal desire for equality while avoiding an examination of white racial privilege or any other privilege.

This book describes how white privilege reinforces the existing racial status quo and overlaps and interacts with other systems of privilege, including those based on gender, sexual orientation, economic wealth, physical ability, and religion. Just as the systems themselves are made invisible by our language, the interaction between the systems is also masked. "People of color, women, gays, and lesbians" are words frequently used to name people who face discrimination. The phrasing suggests that people of color are male, that women are white, and that gays and lesbians have no race, but of course these terms are not mutually exclusive.

Our language, and how we read it, reflects the dominant cultural privileging of whiteness, maleness, and heterosexuality. We cannot combat these default assumptions without identifying race, sex, and sexual orientation more often than we are accustomed to doing. After all, the unwritten rule tells us not to talk about it.

Difficulties also arise with respect to words to describe race, such as "white" and "Black." *The Chicago Manual of Style* uses lowercase letters for the word "Black," and it appears that way in many quotations. Many legal scholars have disagreed with that convention, capitalizing "Black" to show that, as Kimberlè W. Crenshaw explains, "Blacks, like Asians, [and] Latinos . . . constitute a specific cultural group and, (thus) require denotation as a proper noun." Neil Gotanda agrees that "Black" should be capitalized because it "has deep political and social meaning as a liberating term."

Ian Haney López makes a strong argument for also capitalizing the word "white" in his book *White by Law: The Legal Construction of Race*. Nonetheless, because whites usually see ourselves in uppercase letters without even realizing it, because of white privilege, I have declined to capitalize "white" in this text.

Stephanie M. Wildman

Introduction

A colleague of mine once had a dream in which I appeared.[1] My colleague, who is African American, was struggling in this dream to be himself in the presence of a monolithic white maleness that wanted to oppress him and deny his intellect, his humanity, and his right to belong in our community. In his dream, I, a white woman, attempted to speak on his behalf, but the white man and I spoke as if my friend were not there.

This portrayal disturbed me, because I know my friend can speak for himself. Recognizing this fact, he described my discomfort at par-

Earlier versions of this chapter appeared as Stephanie M. Wildman with Adrienne D. Davis, *Language and Silence: Making Systems of Privilege Visible*, 35 SANTA CLARA L. REV. 881 (1995), copyright © 1995 by Stephanie M. Wildman, and in CRITICAL RACE THEORY: THE CUTTING EDGE (ed. Richard Delgado, 1995). Reprinted with permission.

ticipating in a conversation that made him invisible.[2] But I think this portrayal also disturbed me because it made clear my privileged role, a role I had not acknowledged.

My friend was describing the privilege of whiteness that would allow me and the man in the dream to talk about my friend and issues of race in a particular way, between ourselves. Our shared privilege meant that our conversation mattered in terms of whether my friend would ultimately be part of the community. The community was defined by our whiteness, although neither of us articulated that fact or were even necessarily aware of it. The fact that we were both white gave us more than something in common; it gave us the definitive common ground that transcended our differences and gave shape to us as a group with power to define who else would be included in the circle of our community.

In reporting his dream, my friend described me as someone who does not like conflict, a description I found both troubling and inaccurate, but containing a kernel of truth. It is true that I do not *like* conflict. I do not enjoy external or internal conflict; I prefer life flowing smoothly and people getting along with each other. But my life has been about facing internal conflict all the time, although the way I face it is rarely confrontational.

The conflicts I continually face in my life are about privilege. I am committed to finding strategies to combat subordination directed at others. That clarity rarely leads to internal conflict. The conflicts I have faced have not been about oppression or the privileges I do not have, being a woman in a male-dominated society, and being Jewish in a culture that, curiously, is alternatively Christian and nonreligious. Rather, the conflicts are about the privileges I do have, including class, race, and heterosexual privilege, and how to live my life of privilege consonant with my beliefs in equal opportunity and inclusive community.

But I could not have told my friend about these conflicts fifteen years ago, when he told me about his dream, because I would not have described my life, then, as centering on conflicts about privilege: privilege itself is usually invisible to the holder of the privilege. And even if I could have perceived these conflicts, describing privilege as a hardship is a luxury of privilege as well.

We do not perceive privilege as something bestowed on us specially; rather, it appears as the fabric of life, as the way things are. So I could notice if someone treated me differently because I am a woman. I could notice when classes were canceled for Christmas but not for Yom Kippur. But I did not notice the myriad ways in which my white, class, and heterosexual privileges made it easier for me to move in the world.

Then I started to notice.

The importance of friendship in talking about power systems should not be underestimated. In a class I once taught, an African American student observed, "White people always ask me what they can do to fight racism. My answer to them is: Make a friend of color as the first step in this long process."

This advice is important, but I worry about it being misunderstood. For many white people, making a friend of color means they are able to convince themselves that they must not be racist because they have this trophy friend. Another woman of color I know commented that she has many white friends, but avoids discussing race with them. She is afraid of being hurt by her white friends' small stake in issues of race, when her stake is so large. It is easier for her just to avoid the whole conversation.

Given these difficulties, let me say why I am so taken by this simple, yet serious, advice—"Make a friend." Most of us who are white lead lives that are segregated by race. Race is imprinted on most neighborhood patterns, which means it is replicated in schools. Our lives as straight people are generally segregated by sexual orientation also. Most of us who are heterosexual tend to socialize with other heterosexuals, with couples if we ourselves are part of a couple. The lives we lead affect what we can see and hear in the world around us; but we can perceive more of the world through the experiences of those close to us. So if you make a friend across categories of difference, realize that this means working on listening to what is important to your friend.

A university is a special place, offering the opportunity not only to make friends, but also to listen intently to many others who are not friends. This opportunity to hear differing views is particularly important in a law school. Law and justice are symbolic of deeply held values in American culture. In a law school we should be able to think about systems of privilege and the role of law in maintaining or constraining power.

But the power I am concerned with is not the power of an unchecked executive or a runaway Congress. It is the power of privilege maintained by distinct, yet interlocking, power systems. In this book, I address primarily power systems of race, gender, and sexual orientation. I also use examples of other power systems such as class, religious belief, and other-abledness, sometimes called "dis"ability.

I start this examination from some assumptions. I believe everyone reading this book is a person of good faith, who does not *want* to discriminate on the basis of race, sex, sexual orientation, religion, economic wealth, or physical ability. I know bigotry and hatred exist in the world. And it is important for us to combat that kind of ill will. But I assume that people who read a book entitled *Privilege Revealed: How Invisible Preference Undermines America* are trying to "do the right thing" in their daily lives. I want to explain why privilege is so hard to see, even for people of good will.

At a critical legal studies conference on race, a white friend of mine observed that the conference organization had grouped white people with each other to talk about race. "How absurd," she said, "to have white people talk about race only with other white people."

Years later, I now understand that she was half right and half wrong. It is hard for whites to work on our racism alone, because we often do not see the system we uphold. Yet we must work on race and our racism; it is our responsibility, not the job of people of color. Still, because we often cannot see the white privilege that allows us to participate in perpetuating a white supremacist society, we often lack the words to begin this important conversation.

This book seeks to develop the vocabulary needed for an understanding of the interlocking systems of privilege that serve to perpetuate the status quo of privilege and subordination. This vocabulary will aid not only whites but everyone who benefits from systems of privilege.

The jurisprudential focus of the civil rights era has been discrimination. But this focus has not served to change the privilege/subordination status quo. Attacking discrimination alone cannot result in an end to subordination, because systems of privilege regenerate the discriminatory patterns that maintain existing hierarchies of oppression.

We must focus on privilege rather than solely on discrimination if we are to understand racism and hierarchy. This focus also offers a number of concrete conceptual and doctrinal advantages over the discrimination discussion. A discrimination case requires an accusation; in contrast, the statement that "you are privileged" resonates as a fact. Discrimination frequently has to be proven by a showing of intent and causation by a particular perpetrator; proof of privilege does not. A discussion of discrimination places the accuser in a victim-like, subservient status; a discussion of privilege places the focus for change on the privileged actor, where it belongs. Analyzing systems of privilege could give a new direction and energy to jurisprudence about inequality.

Chapter 1, written in cooperation with Adrienne D. Davis, begins with an examination of the language we use to discuss discrimination and subordination, rendering privilege invisible. The chapter then describes the forms of privilege and stresses the importance of examining privilege as well as oppression.

Chapter 2 takes the analysis of privilege into the workplace, a primary domain of antidiscrimination law. This chapter shows how the invisibility of privilege in language creates a false sense of neutrality about the privileged reality of the workplace. Because antidiscrimination law has failed to address privilege, the status quo is perpetuated.

Chapter 3, written by Margalynne Armstrong, examines the operation of systems of privilege in residential housing patterns. The notion of residential "choice" ensures the perpetuation of racial discrimination and the reproduction of privilege.

Chapter 4, authored with Adrienne D. Davis, considers the role of the media in perpetuating systems of privilege. This chapter uses the example of the Clarence Thomas confirmation hearings and Anita Hill's allegation of sexual harassment to illustrate the continuing operation of systems of privilege.

Chapter 5, authored with Trina Grillo, reminds us that the interlocking nature of systems of privilege is not easy to address. It suggests some important pitfalls to avoid when we engage in the conversation about these systems as a step toward transformation.

Chapter 6 continues the theme of transformation, showing how privilege regenerates itself through the unwritten rules of small group dynamics within the context of the legal academy.

Chapter 7 demonstrates through a law and literature lens the role of the rule of law in maintaining systems of privilege, even as an aspiration for justice permeates our culture.

Finally, chapter 8 concludes by considering the importance of discussing the operation of privilege systems in our classrooms. It analyzes the problems and potential of liberatory legal education, which must confront the presence of systems of privilege and the law's role in their perpetuation.

Chapter 1

Stephanie M. Wildman
with Adrienne D. Davis

Making Systems of Privilege Visible

According to Stephen Hawking, the "goal of science is to provide a single theory that describes the whole universe."[1] Because a unified theory has proven so difficult to devise, however, scientists have broken "the problem up into bits and invent[ed] a number of partial theories. Each of these partial theories describes and predicts a certain limited class of observations, neglecting the effects of other[s]."[2] Hawking explains that the general theory of relativity and quantum mechanics, "the great intellectual achievements of the first half of

Earlier versions of this chapter appeared as Stephanie M. Wildman with Adrienne D. Davis, *Language and Silence: Making Systems of Privilege Visible*, 35 SANTA CLARA L. REV. 881 (1995), copyright © 1995 by Stephanie M. Wildman, and in CRITICAL RACE THEORY: THE CUTTING EDGE (ed. Richard Delgado, 1995). Reprinted with permission.

this century," are two such partial theories.[3] "Unfortunately," he elaborates, "these two theories are known to be inconsistent with each other—they cannot both be correct,"[4] and the major endeavor of modern physics has been to unify the two.

While scientists struggle toward the goal of a unified theory of the universe, judges and legal theorists, responding to societal discrimination, have gone in the opposite direction. They have narrowed the law of discrimination to focus only on hostile or discriminatory treatment, often requiring intentional wrongdoing. This narrowing focus is not what the law needs. Legal doctrine needs a unified theory of the dynamics of subordination, one that describes systemic unfairness and recognizes the elements, beyond intent, that lead to and perpetuate discrimination. Before legal thinkers can attempt such a unified theory, we must understand the existence of privilege.

The notion of privilege, although part of the consciousness of popular culture, has not been recognized in legal language and doctrine. This failure to acknowledge privilege, to make it visible in legal doctrine, creates a serious gap in legal reasoning, rendering law unable to address issues of systemic unfairness.

The invisibility of privilege strengthens the power it creates and maintains. The invisible cannot be combated, and as a result privilege is allowed to perpetuate, regenerate, and re-create itself. Privilege is systemic, not an occasional occurrence. Privilege is invisible only until looked for, but silence in the face of privilege sustains its invisibility.

Silence is the lack of sound and voice. Silence may result from a desire for quiet; it may signify intense mental concentration; it may also arise from oppression or fear. Whatever the reason, when there is silence, no criticism is expressed. What we do not say, what we do not talk about, allows the status quo to continue. To describe these unspoken systems means we need to use language. But even when we try to talk about privilege, the language we use inhibits our ability to perceive the systems of privilege that constitute the status quo.

How Language Veils the Existence of Systems of Privilege

Language contributes to the invisibility and regeneration of privilege. To begin the conversation about subordination, we sort ideas into categories such as race and gender. These words are part of a system of categorization that we use without thinking and that seems linguistically neutral. Race and gender are, after all, just words.

Yet when we learn that someone has had a child, our first question is usually "Is it a girl or a boy?" Why do we ask that, instead of something like "Are the mother and child healthy?" We ask, "Is it a girl or a boy?" according to philosopher Marilyn Frye, because we do not know how to relate to this new being without knowing its gender.[5] Imagine how long you could have a discussion with or about someone without knowing her or his gender. We place people into these categories because our world is gendered.

Similarly, our world is also raced, and it is hard for us to avoid taking mental notes as to race. We use our language to categorize by race, particularly, if we are white, when that race is other than white. Marge Shultz has written of calling on a Latino student in her class.[6] She called him Mr. Martínez, but his name was Rodríguez. The class tensed up at her error; earlier that same day another professor had called him Mr. Hernández, the name of the defendant in the criminal law case under discussion. Professor Shultz talked with her class, at its next session, about her error and how our thought processes lead us to categorize in order to think. She acknowledged how this process leads to stereotyping that causes pain to individuals. We all live in this raced and gendered world, inside these powerful categories, that make it hard to see each other as whole people.

But the problem does not stop with the general terms "race" and "gender." Each of these categories contains the images, like an entrance to a tunnel with many passages and arrows pointing down each possible path, of subcategories. Race is often defined as Black and white; sometimes it is defined as white and "of color." There are other races, and sometimes the categories are each listed, for example, as African American, Hispanic American, Asian American, Native American, and White American, if whiteness is mentioned at all. All these words, describing racial subcategories, seem neutral on their face, like equivalent titles. But however the subcategories are listed, however neutrally the words are expressed, these words mask a system of power, and that system privileges whiteness.

Gender, too, is a seemingly neutral category that leads us to imagine subcategories of male and female. A recent scientific article suggested that five genders might be a more accurate characterization of human anatomy, but there is a heavy systemic stake in our image of two genders.[7] The apparently neutral categories male and female mask the privileging of males that is part of the gender power system. Try to think of equivalent gendered titles, like king and queen, prince and princess, and you will quickly see that male and female are not equal titles in our cultural imagination.

Poet and social critic Adrienne Rich has written convincingly about the compulsory heterosexuality that is part of this gender power system.[8] Almost everywhere we look, heterosexuality is portrayed as the norm. In Olympic ice-skating and dancing, for example, a couple is defined as a man partnered with a woman.[9] Heterosexuality is privileged over any other relationship. The words we use, such as "marriage," "husband," and "wife," are not neutral, but convey this privileging of heterosexuality. What is amazing, says Rich, is that there are any lesbians or gay men at all.[10]

Our culture suppresses conversation about class privilege as well as race and gender privileges. Although we must have money or access to money to obtain human necessities such as food, clothing, and shelter, those fundamental needs are recognized only as an individual responsibility. The notion of privilege based on economic wealth is viewed as a radical, dangerous idea, or an idiosyncratic throwback to the past, conjuring up countries with monarchies, nobility, serfs, and peasants. Yet even the archaic vocabulary makes clear that no one wants to be categorized as a have-not. The economic power system is not invisible—everyone knows that money brings privilege. But the myth persists that all have access to that power through individual resourcefulness. This myth of potential economic equality supports the invisibility of the other power systems that prevent fulfillment of that ideal.

Other words we use to describe subordination also mask the operation of privilege. Increasingly, people use terms like "racism" and "sexism" to describe disparate treatment and the perpetuation of power. Yet this vocabulary of "isms" as a descriptive shorthand for undesirable, disadvantaging treatment creates several serious problems.

First, calling someone a racist individualizes the behavior and veils the fact that racism can occur only where it is culturally, socially, and legally supported. It lays the blame on the individual rather than the systemic forces that have shaped that individual and his or her society. White people know they do not want to be labeled racist; they become concerned with how to avoid that label, rather than worrying about systemic racism and how to change it.

Second, the isms language focuses on the larger category, such as race, gender, sexual preference. Isms language suggests that within these larger categories two seemingly neutral halves exist, equal parts in a mirror. Thus Black and white, male and female, heterosexual and gay/lesbian appear, through the linguistic juxtaposition, as equivalent subparts. In fact, although the category does not take note of it, Blacks and whites, men and women, heterosexuals and gays/lesbians are not equivalently situated in society. Thus the way we think and talk about the categories and subcategories that underlie the isms allows us to consider them parallel parts, and obscures the pattern of domination and subordination within each classification.

Similarly, the phrase "isms" itself gives the illusion that all patterns of domination and subordination are the same and interchangeable.

The language suggests that someone subordinated under one form of oppression would be similarly situated to another person subordinated under another form. Thus, a person subordinated under one form may feel no need to view himself/herself as a possible oppressor, or beneficiary of oppression, within a different form. For example, white women, having an ism that defines their condition—sexism—may not look at the way they are privileged by racism. They have defined themselves as one of the oppressed.

Finally, the focus on individual behavior, the seemingly neutral subparts of categories, and the apparent interchangeability underlying the vocabulary of isms all obscure the existence of systems of privilege and power. It is difficult to see and talk about how oppression operates when the vocabulary itself makes these systems of privilege invisible. "White supremacy" is associated with a lunatic fringe, not with the everyday life of well-meaning white citizens. "Racism" is defined by whites in terms of specific, discriminatory racist actions by others. The vocabulary allows us to talk about discrimination and oppression, but it hides the mechanism that makes that oppression possible and efficient. It also hides the existence of specific, identifiable beneficiaries of oppression, who are not always the actual perpetrators of discrimination. The use of isms language, or any focus on discrimination, masks the privileging that is created by these systems of power.

Thus the very vocabulary we use to talk about discrimination obfuscates these power systems and the privilege that is their natural companion. To remedy discrimination effectively we must make the power systems and the privileges they create visible and part of the discourse. To move toward a unified theory of the dynamics of subordination, we have to find a way to talk about privilege. When we discuss race, sex, and sexual orientation, each needs to be described as a power system that creates privileges in some people as well as disadvantages in others. Most of the literature has focused on disadvantage or discrimination, ignoring the element of privilege. To really talk about these issues, privilege must be made visible.

Law plays an important role in the perpetuation of privilege by ignoring that privilege exists. And by ignoring its existence, law, with help from our language, ensures the perpetuation of privilege.

What Is Privilege?

Franklin Language Master Dictionary and Thesaurus—an electronic dictionary with definitions by Merriam-Webster—defines privilege as "a right granted as an advantage or favor." It is true that the holder of a privilege might believe she or he had a right to it, if you tried to take it away. But a right suggests the notion of an entitlement. A privilege is not a right.

The *American Heritage Dictionary of the English Language* (1978) defines privilege as "a special advantage, immunity, permission, right, or benefit granted to or enjoyed by an individual, class, or caste." The word is derived from the Latin *privilegium*, a law affecting an individual. The Latin root *privus* means "single" or "individual," and *lex* means "law." But the legal, systemic nature of the term "privilege" has become lost in its modern meaning. And it is the systemic nature of these power systems that we must begin to examine.

What then is privilege? We all recognize its most blatant forms. "Men only admitted to this club." "We will not allow African Americans into that school." Blatant exercises of privilege certainly exist, but they are not what most people think of as our way of life. They are only the tip of the iceberg, however.

When we try to look at privilege we see several elements. First, the characteristics of the privileged group define the societal norm, often benefiting those in the privileged group. Second, privileged group members can rely on their privilege and avoid objecting to oppression. Both the conflation of privilege with the societal norm and the implicit option to ignore oppression mean that privilege is rarely seen by the holder of the privilege.

A. The Normalization of Privilege

The characteristics and attributes of those who are privileged group members are described as societal norms—as the way things are and as what is normal in society.[11] This normalization of privilege means that members of society are judged, and succeed or fail, measured against the characteristics that are held by those privileged. The privileged characteristic is the norm; those who stand outside are the aberrant or "alternative."

For example, a thirteen-year-old-girl who aspires to be a major-league ballplayer can have only a low expectation of achieving that goal, no matter how superior a batter and fielder she is. Maleness is the foremost "qualification" of major-league baseball players. Similarly, those who legally are permitted to marry are heterosexual. A gay or lesbian couple, prepared to make a life commitment, cannot cross the threshold of qualification to be married.

I had an example of being outside the norm recently when I was called to jury service. Jurors are expected to serve until 5 P.M. During that year, my family's life was set up so that I picked up my children after school at 2:40 and made sure that they got to various activities. If courtroom life were designed to privilege my needs, then there would have been an afternoon recess to honor children. But in this culture children's lives and the lives of their caretakers are the alternative or other, and we must conform to the norm.

Even as these child care needs were outside the norm, I was privileged economically to be able to meet my children's needs. What many would have described as mothering, not privilege—my ability to pick them up and be present in their after-school lives—was a benefit of my association with privilege.

Members of the privileged group gain many benefits by their affiliation with the dominant side of the power system. This affiliation with power is not identified as such; often it may be transformed into and presented as individual merit. Legacy admissions at elite colleges and professional schools are perceived to be merit-based, when this process of identification with power and transmutation into qualifications occurs. Achievements by members of the privileged group are viewed as the result of individual effort, rather than privilege.

Many feminist theorists have described the male tilt to normative standards in law, including the gendered nature of legal reasoning,[12] the male bias inherent in the reasonable person standard,[13] and the gender bias in classrooms.[14] In fact, definitions based on male models delineate many broader societal norms. As Catharine MacKinnon has observed,

> Men's physiology defines most sports, their health needs largely define insurance coverage, their socially designed biographies define workplace expectations and successful career patterns, their perspectives and concerns define quality in scholarship, their experiences and obsessions define merit, their military service defines citizenship, their presence defines family, their inability to get along with each other—their wars and rulerships—defines history, their image defines god, and their genitals define sex.[15]

Male privilege thus defines many vital aspects of American culture from a male point of view. The maleness of that view becomes masked as that view is generalized as the societal norm, the measure for us all.

The use of "he" as a generic pronoun, stated to include all people, but making women in a room invisible when it is used, is seen as a norm. But a generic "she" is not permitted, and many people become upset when women try to use it. This emotion is not about the grammatically correct use of English, but about the challenge to the system of male privilege.

B. Choosing Whether to Struggle against Oppression

Members of privileged groups can opt out of struggles against oppression if they choose. Often this privilege may be exercised by silence. At the same time that I was the outsider in jury service, I was also a privileged insider. During *voir dire*, each prospective juror was asked to introduce herself or himself. The plaintiff's and defendant's attorneys then asked additional questions. I watched the defense attorney, during voir dire, ask each Asian-looking male prospective juror if he spoke English. No one else was asked. The judge did nothing. The Asian American man sitting next to me smiled and flinched as he was asked the question. I wondered how many times in his life he had been made to answer such a question. I considered beginning my own questioning by saying, "I'm Stephanie Wildman, I'm a professor of law, and yes, I speak English." I wanted to focus attention on the subordinating conduct of the attorney, but I did not. I exercised my white privilege by my silence. I exercised my privilege to opt out of engagement, even though this choice may not always be consciously made by someone with privilege.

Depending on the number of privileges someone has, she or he may experience the power of choosing the types of struggles in which to engage. Even this choice may be masked as an identification with oppression, thereby making the privilege that enables the choice invisible.

For example, privilege based on race and class power systems may temper or alleviate gender bias or subordination based on gender. Recently, a white, female federal district court judge said that women should "lighten up a bit on the subject of sexual harassment."[16] This judge urged women to use strategically our sexuality and to enjoy the playfulness and banter of the workplace. The judge who gave this advice has a position of power rooted in her wealthy economic background and her elite connections. She is a sitting federal judge, unlikely to be sexually harassed. And, of course, her race provides a further element of privilege. Examining the world through these lenses of privilege allowed her to confuse her own position of power with the position of all women. By encouraging women to follow her example, this judge acted as though her own economic and racial privilege had not mitigated, in her case, any possible deleterious effect gender bias might have on women in the workplace.

This distorted worldview obscures the privilege that makes it possible. The judge's analysis focused on her gender, a potential source of subordination, and ignored all the benefits she had accrued by virtue of her class and race privilege. The holder of privilege may enjoy deference, special knowledge, or a higher comfort level to guide societal interaction. Privilege is not visible to its holder; it is merely there, a part of the world, a way of life, simply the way things are. Others have a *lack*, an absence, a deficiency.

Systems of Privilege

Although different privileges bestow certain common characteristics (membership in the norm, the ability to choose whether to object to the power system, and the invisibility of its benefit), the form of a privilege may vary according to the power relationship that produces it. White privilege derives from the race power system of white supremacy. Male privilege[17] and heterosexual privilege result from the gender hierarchy.[18] Class privilege derives from an economic, wealth-based hierarchy.

Examining white privilege from the perspective of one who benefits from it, Peggy McIntosh has found it "an elusive and fugitive subject. The pressure to avoid it is great."[19] She defines white privilege as

an invisible package of unearned assets which [she] can count on cashing in each day, but about which [she] was "meant" to remain oblivious.[20] White privilege is like an invisible weightless knapsack of special provisions, assurance, tools, maps,

guides, codebooks, passports, visas, clothes, compass, emergency gear, and blank checks.[21]

McIntosh identified forty-six advantages available to her as a white
person that her African American coworkers, friends, and acquain-
tances could not count on.[22] Some of these include being told that
people of her color made American heritage or civilization what it is;
not needing to educate her children to be aware of systemic racism
for their own daily protection; and never being asked to speak for all
people of her racial group.[23]

Different advantages accrue from society's privileging of heterosexuality, which generally constitutes gay and lesbian relations as
invisible.[24] Marc Fajer describes what he calls three societal pre-
understandings about gay men and lesbians: the sex-as-lifestyle
assumption, the cross-gender assumption, and the idea that gay
issues are inappropriate for public discussion.

According to Fajer, the sex-as-lifestyle assumption is the "common
non-gay belief that gay people experience sexual activity differently
from non-gays" in a way that is "all-encompassing, obsessive and
completely divorced from love, long-term relationships, and family
structure."[25] As to the cross-gender assumption, Fajer explains that
many nongay people believe that gay men and lesbians exhibit
"behavior stereotypically associated with the other gender."[26] The
idea that gay issues are inappropriate for public discussion has
received prominent press coverage recently as "Don't ask, don't tell"
concerning the military.[27] Thus, even if being gay is acceptable, "talking about being gay is not," according to Fajer.[28] One professor I
know has a picture of his lover of twenty years, who is also male, on
his desk, along with a photo of their son. No one has ever said to him,
"What a lovely family you have."

Fajer does not discuss these pre-understandings explicitly in terms
of privilege. Nevertheless, he is describing the sexual orientation

power system that privileges heterosexuals: they function in a world where negative assumptions are not made about their sexuality, and their sexuality may be discussed and even advertised in public.

The identification of class structures and class privilege is problematic in modern American society because of the myth that the United States is a classless society; the existence of the class-based power system itself is denied. Discrimination based on race, sex, and other power systems is considered illegal, but discrimination based on wealth has been interpreted as permissible by the Constitution. In a society where basic human needs, such as food, clothing, and shelter, can be met only with money, the privilege of class and wealth seems clear.

In spite of the pervasiveness of privilege, it is interesting that antidiscrimination practice and theory have generally not examined privilege and its role in perpetuating discrimination. One notable exception is Kimberlè Crenshaw, who has explained, using the examples of race and sex, that

> Race and sex . . . become significant only when they operate to explicitly *disadvantage* the victims; because the *privileging* of whiteness or maleness is implicit, it is generally not perceived at all.[29]

Antidiscrimination advocates focus only on one portion of the power system, the subordinated characteristic, rather than seeing the essential links between domination, subordination, and the resulting privilege.

Adrienne Davis writes:

> Domination, subordination, and privilege are like three heads of a hydra. Attacking the most visible heads, domination and subordination, trying bravely to chop them up into little pieces,

> will not kill the third head, privilege. Like a mythic multi-head-
> ed hydra, which will inevitably grow another head if all heads
> are not slain, discrimination cannot be ended by focusing only
> on . . . subordination and domination.[30]

Subordination will grow back from the ignored head of privilege, yet
the descriptive vocabulary and conceptualization of discrimination
hinders our ability to see the hydra head of privilege. This invisibility is serious, because what is not seen cannot be discussed or
changed. Thus to end subordination, one must first recognize privilege. Seeing privilege means articulating a new vocabulary and structure for antisubordination theory. Only by visualizing this privilege
and incorporating it into discourse can people of good faith combat
discrimination.

Visualizing Privilege

For me the struggle to visualize privilege has most often taken the
form of the struggle to see my white privilege. Even as I write about
this struggle, I fear that my own racism will make things worse, caus-
ing me to do more harm than good. Some readers may be shocked to
see a white person contritely acknowledge that she is racist. I do not
say this with pride. I simply believe that no matter how hard I work
at not being racist, I still am. Because part of racism is systemic, I
benefit from the privilege that I am struggling to see.

Whites do not look at the world through a filter of racial awareness, even though whites are, of course, members of a race. The
power to ignore race, when white is the race, is a privilege, a societal
advantage. The term "racism/white supremacy" emphasizes the link
between discriminatory racism and the privilege held by whites to
ignore their own race.

As bell hooks explains, liberal whites do not see themselves as prejudiced or interested in domination through coercion, yet "they can-

not recognize the ways their actions support and affirm the very structure of racist domination and oppression that they profess to wish to see eradicated."[31] The perpetuation of white supremacy is racist.

All whites are racist in this use of the term, because we benefit from systemic white privilege. Generally whites think of racism as voluntary, intentional conduct, done by horrible others. Whites spend a lot of time trying to convince ourselves and each other that we are not racist. A big step would be for whites to admit that we are racist and then to consider what to do about it.[32]

I also work on not being sexist. This work is different from my work on my racism, because I am a woman and I experience gender subordination. But it is important to realize that even when we are not privileged by a particular power system, we are products of the culture that instills its attitudes in us. I have to make sure that I am calling on women students and listening to them as carefully as I listen to men.

While we work at seeing privilege, it is also important to remember that each of us is much more complex than simply our race and gender. Just as I have a race, which is white, and a gender, which is female, I have a sexual orientation (heterosexual at this time) and religious beliefs (I am Jewish), I have thin fingers, I am a swimmer, and so forth.

The point is that I am, and all of us are, lots of things. Kimberlè Crenshaw introduced the idea of the intersection into feminist jurisprudence.[33] Her work examines the intersection of race, as African American, with gender as female. Thus Crenshaw's intersectionality analysis focused on intersections of subordination. Privilege can intersect with subordination or other systems of privilege as well.

Seeing privilege at the intersection is complicated by the fact that there is no purely privileged or unprivileged person. Most of us are privileged in some ways and not in others. A very poor person might have been the oldest child in the family and exercised power over his siblings. The wealthiest African American woman, who could be a federal judge, might still have racial, sexist epithets hurled at her as she walks down the street. The experience of both privilege and subordination in different aspects of our lives causes the experiences to be blurred, and the presence of privilege is further hidden from our vocabulary and consciousness.

Often we focus on the experience of oppression and act from privilege to combat that oppression without consciously making that choice. An African American woman professor may act from the privilege of power as a professor to overcome the subordination her white male students would otherwise seek to impose on her. Or a white female professor may use the privilege of whiteness to define the community of her classroom, acting from the power of that privilege to minimize any gender disadvantage that her students would use to undermine her classroom control. Because the choice to act from privilege may be unconscious, the individual, for example, the white female professor, may see herself as a victim of gender discrimination, which she may in fact be. But she is unlikely to see herself as a participant in discrimination for utilizing her white privilege to create the classroom environment.

Intersectionality can help reveal privilege, especially when we remember that the intersection is multidimensional, including intersections of both subordination and privilege. Imagine intersections in three dimensions, where multiple lines intersect. From the center one can see in many different directions. Every individual exists at the center of these multiple intersections, where many strands meet, similar to a Koosh ball.[34]

The Koosh ball is a popular children's toy. Although it is called a ball and that category leads one to imagine a firm, round object used for catching and throwing, the Koosh ball is neither hard nor firm.

Picture hundreds of rubber bands, tied in the center. Mentally cut the end of each band. The wriggling, unfirm mass in your hand is a Koosh ball, still usable for throwing and catching, but changing shape as it sails through the air or as the wind blows through its rubbery limbs when it is at rest. It is a dynamic ball.

The Koosh ball is the perfect postmodern ball. Its image "highlights that each person is embedded in a matrix of . . . [categories] that interact in different contexts" taking different shapes.[35] In some contexts we are privileged and in some subordinated, and these contexts interact. The Koosh ball metaphor is a step toward a unified theory of subordination because it illustrates the mutating nature of the systems of privilege as they interact within and between individuals.

Even the words we use to describe systems of privilege are dynamic in the same way the Koosh ball is. For example, when society categorizes someone on the basis of race, as either white or of color, it picks up a strand of the Koosh, a piece of rubber band, and says, "See this strand, this is defining and central. It matters." Even naming the experience "race" veils its many facets, because race may be a whole cluster of strands, including color, culture, identification, and experience. Race might be a highly important strand, but isolating one thread does not allow the shape of the whole ball or the whole person to emerge.

This tendency to label with categories obfuscates our vision of the whole Koosh ball, where multiple strands interrelate. No individual really fits into any one category; rather, everyone resides at the intersection of many categories. Categorical thinking makes it hard or impossible to conceptualize the complexity of an individual. The cultural push has long been to choose a category.[36] Yet forcing a choice results in a hollow vision that cannot do justice.

Justice requires that we see the whole person in her or his social context, but the social contexts are complicated. Subordination cannot be adequately described with ordinary language, because that language masks privilege and makes the bases of subordination themselves appear linguistically neutral. As a result the hierarchy of power implicit in words such as "race," "gender," and "sexual orientation" is banished from the language. Once the hierarchy is made visible, the problems remain no less complex, but it becomes possible to discuss them in a more revealing and useful fashion.

Chapter 2

Stephanie M. Wildman

Privilege in the Workplace
The Missing Element in Antidiscrimination Law

The workplace presents an example of how supposedly neutral language—the very words we use to describe work and what occurs
there—masks systems of privilege. The invisibility of privilege in the
workplace perpetuates the systemic nature of disadvantage. With
Title VII of the 1964 Civil Rights Act, federal law aimed at ending
workplace segregation by focusing on discrimination in employment. However, antidiscrimination doctrine developed under this
statute has ignored privilege, ensuring the replication of systems of
subordination. The resulting denial of access to jobs and promotions

An earlier version of this chapter appeared as Stephanie M. Wildman, *Privilege in the Workplace: The Missing Element in Anti-Discrimination Law*, 4 TEXAS JOURNAL OF WOMEN AND THE LAW 171 (1995), copyright © 1995 by Stephanie M. Wildman.

serves to maintain existing economic disparity that income would alleviate.

The Normalization of Privilege in the Workplace

Envision the heretofore invisible systems of privilege in the workplace by considering the example of women. When we think about women and the workplace we should imagine the whole earth, because indeed women work everywhere. Yet somehow our definition of work is attached to a location we call the workplace. Even the recent wave of feminism in the 1970s encountered difficulty with the rhetoric of work, and women who work in the home felt left out of its movement. But the idea of women's work, as the domestic sphere, and men's work, as the real work in the so-called public sphere, has been deeply entrenched in our language and culture. White middle-class women are entering the world of work outside the home in increasing numbers. Many women of color and working-class women have long worked outside their homes. At this historic time we need to expand the notion of work and the definition of where it is done, promoting a vision of women at work everywhere we do work.

When we contrast this vision of the wholeness of women's work, permeating all aspects of life, including giving life itself, with the narrower legal vision of workplace, the kind of place covered by federal and state antidiscrimination laws, we can begin to see the limits of law's vision. This narrowness is necessarily ours as well, we who work within the law. But we must push on that boundary, narrowly drawn to meet our cultural definition of work, and give it elasticity. Keeping this larger vision of women as workers throughout the world in mind can help us see what is missing from antidiscrimination law.

To be in the workplace is to enter a male-defined world. Even the notion of a workplace, which exists outside the home, privileges maleness, associating work with male values and culture. This privileging of maleness in the workplace has not stopped simply because women now work there as well.[1]

Thus, although "workplace" is an apparently neutral term, descriptive of a place of work, it has a male tilt to it. The notion of "workplace" divides the earth into loci of work and nonwork, defining only what occurs in a workplace as work. This idea of workplace as a neutral ideal permeates our cultural thinking and obscures the male point of view it embodies.[2]

How women are treated and how we should behave in the workplace—that particular location we have designated as the locus where work occurs—are contested and negotiated in many places outside the workplace.[3] These locations, although spatially separate, interconnect as spheres of influence on the definition of woman. How male workers relate to their mothers, sisters, and daughters influences how they see and relate to women at work. If these workers are used to having their views privileged at home and then receive different treatment from women in the work environment, they may perceive their women coworkers as "not doing a good job." If women are smiling and compliant in the media, then that view also may be carried over into workplace expectations.

Recently, space geographers (scholars examining the social construction of place) have pointed out the gendered nature of space;[4] they have found that segregated space correlates to lack of power and knowledge on the part of the excluded group.[5] Women do work everywhere, yet the culture does not always define that labor as work. Work performed in sex-segregated isolation, such as in the domestic sphere, is a prime example of hard work that is neither recognized nor compensated.

The privileging that occurs in the workplace does not stop at maleness. Whiteness, heterosexuality, and middle-class values are all privileged in the workplace, as they are privileged in our culture. This privileging is rarely acknowledged or recognized: the dominant culture proclaims that the workplace is a situs of neutral values and judgments based on merit and performance. But that very claim of neutrality, often heartily believed, masks the values it privileges.[6]

Viewed through this lens of neutrality, workers are equivalent and interchangeable. The U.S. Supreme Court canonized the notion of interchangeable workers when it introduced the term "non-pregnant person" into early employment discrimination litigation. The Court declared that it was not sex discrimination to disadvantage pregnant workers.[7] Nonpregnant persons included women and men, the Court reasoned, implying that they were interchangeable in relation to pregnancy. In treating all workers the same in relation to pregnancy, the Court promoted the idea of the workplace as neutral.

An awareness of privilege is missing from our cultural vision of the workplace. This inability to identify and articulate privilege is also missing from antidiscrimination law as it is applied to the workplace. Antidiscrimination law has not addressed privilege, the flip side of disadvantaging, subordinate treatment. As I noted earlier, the jurisprudential focus of the civil rights era has been discrimination. But attacking discrimination alone cannot end subordination, because systems of privilege regenerate the discriminatory patterns that maintain the existing hierarchies of oppression.

Title VII law has missed the systemic nature of the discrimination it seeks to combat, and, therefore, failed to provide a remedy. In naming sex, race, national origin, color, and religion, Title VII articulates categories to be particularly scrutinized in a search for unfair treatment in the workplace. Case law development under Title VII has focused on discrimination based on these categories, but not on the power systems that operate within and across each category to discriminate against some and privilege many.[8] This deficiency in Title VII doctrine, ignoring the operation of privilege, has handicapped antidiscrimination law and doomed it to failure.

Privilege, as chapter 1 explained, is the systemic conferral of benefit and advantage. Members of a privileged group gain this status by affiliation, conscious or not and chosen or not, to the dominant side of a power system. The Title VII categories identify power systems. At a recent conference, Professor Frances Ansley drew a horizontal line, labeled the power line, and asked participants to imagine where they were situated in terms of race, gender, sexual orientation, and other categories. Everyone knew what she meant by the power line, which divided those attributes that are privileged from those that are not. Those above the power line shared privileged characteristics.

Affiliation with the dominant side of the power line is often defined as merit and worthiness. Characteristics and behaviors shared by those on the dominant side of the power line often delineate the societal norm. For example, white skin color is often called "flesh-colored"; women's hosiery colors labeled "nude" are also a pale tone. Human skin comes in many different colors and shades, but whiteness is privileged to have the definition of human color associated with it. Hiring someone with an English or German accent, who is difficult to understand, may be acceptable; the accent is associated with upper-class and European privilege. But hiring someone with a Filipino accent may bring the criticism that the person cannot speak English.[9] A loud, deep voice is privileged in public speaking, such as in law school teaching. One law professor I know was told on her evaluations that she would be a better teacher if she lowered her voice an octave. Women's voices are often described pejoratively as "high and squeaky," but we do not have negative words to describe a low-pitched voice. Even "booming" is complimentary.

As I pointed out in chapter 1, the holder of privilege can opt in or out of struggles against oppression, again often unconsciously. What is more, a privileged person may be silent in the face of some forms of oppression even while believing that she is fighting oppression when it appears in another form. Heterosexual white women are often unconscious of our sexual orientation and race privileges and the ways we perpetuate heterosexism and racism even while we are fighting sexism.

Perhaps most important, privilege is not visible to the holder of the privilege; privilege appears as part of the normal fabric of daily life, not as something special. Privilege often bestows a higher comfort level in social interaction; the holder of privilege need not feel excluded when the norm describes her own actuality. One diversity consultant uses this example:

> Suppose you as a human are told to live in the ocean in a society of fish. You find it difficult to breathe. When you complain that oxygen is a problem, the fish would say this is simply the way the world is, and you should adjust. The fish might even feel beleaguered as you gasp. "You are getting tiresome," they say, "can't you think of *anything* besides oxygen?" Water is the only world they know, even though the fish did not create it.[10]

People of color and white women must learn the workplace world of white male supremacy, which they did not create, and master how to live in it, even though it deprives them of the equivalent of oxygen. Well-meaning people who function in that world as white males, like the fish, think that their world is normal, the way things are. For the most part, they do not mean to discriminate or disadvantage.

Title VII of the Civil Rights Act and Its Limitations

If everyone were simply privileged or just subordinated, then the analysis of systems of privilege would be easier. But each of us lives at the juncture of privilege in some areas and subordination in others. The Koosh ball image explained in chapter 1 describes this reality of three-dimensional intersection. The rubbery strands of the Koosh ball consist of threads of both subordination and privilege. In some contexts we are privileged and in some subordinated, and these contexts interact. Nonetheless, some systems of privilege are more socially significant than others.

Thus the problem discrimination law must address is too complex to be solved by selecting a single basis for unfair treatment, as urged by the statutory language. Privilege must be analyzed along with disadvantaging treatment. A re-examination of Title VII of the 1964 Civil Rights Act illustrates the limitations of the statute in acknowledging the complexity of systems of privilege.

Federal antidiscrimination law has been described as "a patchwork of statutes and one major executive order."[11] Although Title VII is only a piece of this patchwork, it is the "centerpiece" of federal employment discrimination law, and interpretations of Title VII are often applied to other antidiscrimination statutes.

Title VII forbids an employer to "fail or refuse to hire or to discharge any individual, or *otherwise to discriminate* against any individual with respect to his [*sic*] compensation, terms, conditions, or privileges of employment," or to "limit, segregate, or classify his [*sic*] employees or applicants for employment *in any way* which would deprive or tend to deprive any individual of employment opportunities or otherwise adversely affect his [*sic*] status as an employee, because of such individual's race, color, religion, sex, or national origin."[12] This language has been interpreted to mean that intentional discrimination based on the forbidden classifications is illegal,[13] and actions having a disparate impact may be illegal as well.[14]

Given that language tends toward categorization as an intrinsic part of naming, it is unlikely that any new statute could avoid the pitfalls of categories. A new statute is not necessary because the language forbidding an employer from *limiting* an employee or applicant because of any illegal classification could be used to encompass limits imposed because of the existence of systems of privilege. So the statutory language of Title VII could be used to encompass a vision of a workplace that did not privilege maleness, or any other system above the power line, even though Title VII case law has not developed in this manner.

We have come a long way since 1964, when the Civil Rights Act was passed and gender was added on the Senate floor as a joke, as a way to sabotage the bill. The 1970s were marked by litigation that stressed formal equality, when women sought treatment equivalent to men's. During that period women said, "Just give us a chance to be estate administrators or derive benefits from the armed service. We can do the job as well as men can." And the doors opened a bit.

But even the women's community quickly began debating the limits of formal equality. The discussion about the treatment of pregnancy, called equal/special or equal/accommodation debate, depending on one's view of the resolution, highlighted the interpretive nature of equality theory. The lesson emerged from the pregnancy debate that we all view the world from a particular perspective that affects what we are able to perceive. And so not surprisingly, feminist legal theorists turned to context with increased intensity. The anti-essentialism movement of the last decade has increased our wariness toward generalization and our fondness for particularity. Women of color have taught us that antidiscrimination law has failed to look at the intersections of subordination, thereby missing altogether the meaning of the discrimination they experience.

During these developments in feminist legal theory, Title VII doctrine has evolved in a direction adverse to discrimination plaintiffs' interests. In her description of Title VII's history, Martha West explains, "Since 1981, the Court has interpreted Title VII in ways that have created additional obstacles for plaintiffs, not just women, but all Title VII plaintiffs."[15] West continues to explain four "restrictive and unnecessary constructions" by courts that have undercut the possible effectiveness of Title VII as an antidiscrimination statute. These constructions include the focus on employer discriminatory intent, the need to show that such intent was a motivating factor in the decision, the allowance that employers may prove that the same result would have occurred absent the discrimination, and the view that discriminatory intent is a question of fact, inhibiting possible judicial review.[16]

West recognizes the existence of subconscious, unintentional discrimination and complains that the law has not developed in ways that are able to remedy that discrimination and its effects. Describing discrimination as "the product of widely-held, but often unarticulated prejudices and assumptions," West acknowledges that discrimination has a systemic nature. That systemic nature includes the usually unseen hydra head of privilege. The recognition of systems of privilege, complementing these systems of discrimination, would provide the legal system with a full picture of the dynamic of subordination.

Title VII says it is illegal to "otherwise discriminate" or to "limit . . . employees . . . in any way." This statutory language is broad enough to include an analysis of invisible systems of privilege and power, which operate based on sex, race, national origin, color, or religion to deprive individuals of employment opportunities. Systems of privilege and power, by privileging those with certain characteristics or behaviors, are "limiting" individuals who lack those characteristics and behaviors.

In addition, if only one system of privilege and power is addressed, potential litigants will be unable to describe the complexity of the privilege and subordination dynamic. Systems of privilege and subordination interact with each other within the workplace. An individual white lesbian may be disadvantaged by the heterosexual workplace culture, which Title VII does not explicitly prohibit. Yet that heterosexual culture is so connected to definitions of maleness and femaleness that her disadvantaging may not be separable from the privileging of maleness at work, which limits the worker on account of her sex.

The statutory language of Title VII, as it is written, helps mask the existence and interaction of these systems of privilege and power. Several problems are created by the statutory language: (1) the analogy problem, which implies the fungibility of the categories; (2) the comparison mode, by which statutory language and case law tend to compare treatment of the discrimination plaintiff to treatment of another individual with characteristics or behaviors on the other side of the power line of a particular classification; and (3) perhaps primarily, the invisibility of privilege at all in either statutory language, case law development, or cultural consciousness.

A. The Analogy Problem in Statutory Drafting

Title VII of the 1964 Civil Rights Act, which has served as a model antidiscrimination statute forbidding discrimination in employment, illustrates how the statutory drafting implicitly analogizes the discrimination of one group to that of another. Title VII lists "race, color, religion, sex, or national origin"[17] as the categories for which discrimination is forbidden. The goal of combating discrimination in all these areas should be applauded. Yet the effect of this laundry list of groups, against whom discrimination is forbidden, implies a similarity between them, as well as shared characteristics that distinguish them from other groups not mentioned. The absence of a prohibition from discrimination against lesbians and gay men is a serious omission.

The implicit emphasis on the similarities of the harm suffered from the various types of discrimination obscures the question of how those harms might be different. While the difference in the harms might not mean that the law should remedy them differently, the exploration of those questions has not even been attempted and is implicitly discouraged. Differences in the harms are simply ignored; the categories are viewed as fungible. A Black man hired to lead a public interest organization was told by a white woman, "I'm upset you got this job, when there was a qualified woman." The woman to whom she referred was white. The woman's comment suggests she believed it would have been the same act for the organization to hire a Black man, a white woman, or perhaps even a woman of color for the leadership position. But hiring a white woman would have done nothing to change the system of white supremacy; it would have only combated the system of male dominance. To imply that these systems are the same ignores important realities of both forms of oppression in the workplace and in the culture that sustains it.

Just as the forms of oppression and discrimination are different, the privileging based on each statutory categorization takes place in different ways. The differences are made harder to see because of the implicit fungibility in the statute, which makes all categories seem equivalent. In the workplace, whiteness and maleness may both be privileged as attributes of a leader, but sexual orientation, when it is heterosexual, is not regarded. This perceived invisibility of sexual orientation privileges heterosexuality. Yet heterosexuality is very visible when workers display pictures of spouse and family. But visible displays of sexuality are usually acceptable only for heterosexual workers. Many gay and lesbian workers do not feel safe displaying photos of their families in their work environments.

B. The Comparison Mode Veils the Operation of Privilege

The comparison mode has been used by an individual claiming disparate, disadvantaging treatment by comparing the treatment of the individual to treatment received by those in another social group. For example, a woman barred from the practice of law claimed that men could practice law and, therefore, she should be admitted to practice. The comparison mode, however, veils the operation of privilege. Many cases involving discrimination based on gender, race, and other Title VII categories will never be brought because the Title VII analysis has been based on a comparison mode.[18]

In employment discrimination cases, a plaintiff claiming discrimination based on sex must show how men were treated differently in the workplace.[19] For example, one court has said, "It is significant to note that instances of complained of sexual conduct that prove equally offensive to male and female workers would not support a Title VII sexual harassment charge because both men and women were accorded like treatment."[20] Yet offensive sexual conduct in the workplace supports a system of subordination of women by men that contravenes the goal of equal employment embodied in Title VII.[21]

Privileging of whiteness in the workplace can occur even when all participants are African American. This privileging will remain invisible under the comparison mode. One litigator I know described a case that settled in which the African American female plaintiff sued for discrimination under Title VII. Her supervisor was a white woman, but the other coworkers in her department were also African American women.

The plaintiff was a large, dark, and loud woman. The supervisor was small and demure. The plaintiff could not prove discrimination under Title VII, which would compare her situation to others. The evidence that other African American women were employed in her workplace would dispel her claim of race discrimination. That she was the "wrong kind" of African American woman, because of societal preference for certain characteristics, could not be remedied under the statutory framework without an analysis of privilege.

The poverty of the comparison mode has been further demonstrated by feminist critical race scholars such as Kimberlè Crenshaw, Paulette Caldwell, and Elvia Arriola,[22] who explain that African

American women are rendered invisible by such comparative thinking. Cases have found that they are not Black for race discrimination purposes and not women for sex discrimination purposes.[23] By this comparative logic, discrimination against women of color is placed beyond the reach of the statute.

C. The Invisibility of Privilege

Finally, the invisibility of privilege is perhaps the most pernicious flaw in antidiscrimination doctrine. Certain work is neither defined as work nor seen as significant or meritorious in job performance. Caring for people is a significant aspect of work that is not valued in many workplaces.

For example, one administrator does the work of three people, but she is not paid accordingly. She cannot demonstrate sex discrimination: there is no similarly situated male administrator in her department. So under the comparison mode, she has no case, and she does have a job, so there was no discrimination in hiring. Her employer was willing to hire a woman. The employer would say, "We are employing a woman, so how can we be discriminating based on sex?" But much of this administrator's work requires caring for people within the institution, being sure that their needs are met in myriad ways. This work is invisible work; it would never appear in a job description. Meeting needs and keeping people happy are tasks women do outside the workplace, in the home. When women arrive in the workplace, the gendered expectation is that they will still perform that caretaking role. Yet that caretaking role is not privileged.

In the era before the political year of the woman, a colleague told me the following joke. He asked whether I knew why Congress did not get more accomplished. When I asked him why, he replied, "Because there aren't enough women in it." This "joke" illustrates some of the cultural complexities related to gender and workplace interaction. My colleague was trying to let me know that women do all the dirty work; they are the ones who get things done. But they presumably do that job in an uncomplaining, quiet, unseen way. He tells the story as a joke, but its humor requires that all of us understand the unrecognized work women do. Laughter may recognize but does not help to change the undervaluation of women's contributions.

The invisibility of privilege within Title VII doctrine is evidenced in *Price Waterhouse v. Hopkins.*[24] In *Price Waterhouse*, a woman's partnership candidacy in an accounting firm was held for reconsideration. Later, the partners in her office refused to repropose her candidacy, and she sued under Title VII, claiming that the partnership process had discriminated against her on the basis of sex. Although the U.S. Supreme Court decision focused on the appropriate burden of proof in cases where an employment decision resulted from a mixture of legitimate and illegitimate motives, the case is useful for purposes of this essay for its discussion of sex stereotyping in decision making.

Plaintiff Hopkins was seen very differently by different partners. In one document she was described as "'an outstanding professional' who had a 'deft touch,' a 'strong character, independence and integrity.'" Her interpersonal skills received negative comments, however, and she was described as "sometimes overly aggressive, unduly harsh, difficult to work with, and impatient with staff." Interestingly, the Supreme Court apparently did not consider this comment gender-related, and it continued in the next sentence to say that some partners reacted negatively to Hopkins's personality because she was a woman. We can only speculate as to whether a man who behaved as Hopkins did would be described as "overly aggressive, unduly harsh, and difficult to work with," or whether he would be described as having rough edges in his enthusiasm to get the job done and as someone who needed seasoning.

But even the Supreme Court could not miss the gender stereotyping at work when one partner advised that plaintiff should "walk more femininely, talk more femininely, dress more femininely, wear make-up, have her hair styled, and wear jewelry." Hopkins was obviously being criticized for not meeting a stereotyped notion of femininity. However, one can imagine another employment situation where a woman who used makeup and jewelry, conforming to this notion of attractiveness, could be told that she did not conform to the company's professional image. Discrimination means women cannot win; whatever they do is wrong because they are not men. For women discrimination means lose-lose.

The problem in the Supreme Court's analysis of sex stereotyping is that it examines only discrimination and ignores privilege. A system of male privilege means that men are setting the standard to which women must conform. They are determining what kind of woman is the "right kind." If you behave at work in one particular way, you may be out; but if you perform in the other manner, you might still have a problem. An analysis of privilege that goes beyond simply stereotyping is necessary to examine the gender power system and how decisions based on it in the workplace harm women.[25]

In a recent visit to Title VII,[26] the U.S. Supreme Court further narrowed the legal requirements for proving discrimination. This interpretation has taken the Court a step further in the wrong direction as the Court ignores the dynamics of subordination and fails to see the operation of white privilege, even as the Court itself privileges whiteness in the language of the decision.

In the case, plaintiff Melvin Hicks sued his employer, St. Mary's Honor Center, a halfway house operated by the Missouri Department of Corrections, alleging intentional race discrimination.[27] According to the Court, Hicks had a satisfactory employment record until John Powell became his supervisor, and Steve Long became the new superintendent. Hicks became the subject of "repeated, and increasingly severe, disciplinary actions. He was suspended for five days . . . . He received a letter of reprimand. . . . He was later demoted from shift commander to correctional officer. . . . Finally he was discharged for threatening Powell during an exchange of heated words."

In its description of the facts of the case in the second and third paragraph of the opinion, the Court describes Hicks as "a black man." Evidently the Court believes it is appropriate to mention race because this case involves race discrimination. But the Supreme Court does not mention Powell's or Long's race, which might also be relevant. By its omission, the Court invites the reader to assume that their race is white, making white race the default, the norm, the privileged race.[28]

In contrast, the trial court opinion, in frequent footnotes, does designate race, stating that Powell is white, but curiously omitting Long.[29] The court of appeals decision states that "Long and Powell are both white."[30] The absence of references to whiteness by the U.S. Supreme Court in its description of actors in the *Hicks* drama demonstrates the privileging of whiteness, not only in the workplace, but in the culture in which that workplace is being contested. But that privileging is not even visible to the Court itself.

The Supreme Court cites with approval the district court conclusion that "although [respondent] had proven the existence of a crusade to terminate him, he has not proven that the crusade was racially rather than personally motivated."[31] This separation of the racial from the personal is curious. The Court ignores race as a part of what a human "personally" is. This separation of our beings from our work identity contributes to the male tilt evidenced in the workplace. And to the extent the world is raced, it is hard to imagine that privileging whiteness played no part in the workplace drama that resulted in Hicks's termination. A failure to evaluate the whole picture surrounding a job termination cannot be justice.

In the next chapter, Margalynne Armstrong describes the role of economic disparity in residential segregation. The workplace is one location where economic disparities could be changed: access to work directly affects economic power. But the systems of privilege that she describes in the housing sphere exist in the workplace as well. Thus far, these systems have been insulated not only from Title VII review but also from the vocabulary of our cultural consciousness.

The 1970s feminist slogan "The personal is political" remains true. This slogan recognized the poverty of the private/public dichotomy that separated spheres of work from our spheres of life. We need to remember that the personal is part of our work and that where and how we work is very personal. We can start by looking in the mirror and examining the privileges we each have.

Chapter 3

Margalynne Armstrong

Privilege in Residential Housing

Few things feel more personal than the choice of where we live and whom we live with. And few things are more devastating than being denied that choice because of race discrimination. Okainer Christian Dark describes the experience of housing discrimination (she was excluded from renting an apartment because she is African American) as "someone taking a piece of paper with everything on it that describes you—more than a resume, because it includes your essence—and crumpling it up because the reader didn't like the color." She says she is still trying to smooth out the

An earlier version of this chapter appeared as Margalynne Armstrong, *Protecting Privilege: Race, Residence and Rodney King*, 12 LAW & INEQUALITY: A JOURNAL OF THEORY AND PRACTICE 351 (1994), copyright © 1994 by Law & Inequality: A Journal of Theory and Practice. Reprinted with permission.

paper, but it can never be the same as it was before it got the wrinkles.

Professor Dark also describes her two-year-old son, who will soon have to learn how to respond to race discrimination, and how she will have to teach him how to react. White children do not have to learn this lesson, and their parents do not have to worry about teaching their children how to respond to this assault on their essential being. In fact, most white families are insulated from understanding that African American parents must teach these lessons, because we live in communities isolated from each other. This ignorance is another aspect of white privilege.

The 1992 acquittal of the Los Angeles police officers who beat Rodney King and the resulting devastation of an already ravaged community raised in stark relief this issue of where Americans reside and how those "choices" come to be made. The America represented by Rodney King and South Central Los Angeles lives in segregated cities, while the America of the police defendants and Ventura County jurors resides in segregated suburbs.[1] "Two nations" is a recurring metaphor for the racial configuration of the United States.[2]

Metropolitan residential patterns reflect widely held convictions that "good neighborhoods" exclude poor Blacks and Latinos. The segregation of poor minorities, particularly African Americans, in urban ghettos exacerbates their poverty and creates a false sense that urban problems are not the concern of suburban residents. But the suburbs are not insulated from urban crises: "The real city is the total metropolitan area—city and suburb."[3] The urban inner city and outlying suburbs will inevitably clash because American society cannot back away from its proclamations that the segregation that sustains these contrasting worlds will no longer be tolerated.

According to our nation's Constitution and the Fair Housing Act, both governmental and privately imposed discrimination are prohibited. The Fair Housing Act, enacted in 1968, provides that it is unlawful "to discriminate against any person in the terms, conditions or privileges of sale or rental of a dwelling . . . because of race, color, religion, sex, familial status or national origin."[4] But despite this broad mandate, the law has been interpreted to reach only a narrow spectrum of racial exclusion. The law provides no redress for much of the widespread segregation of poor minority Americans committed under the auspices of privilege, both racial and economic.

Rather than prohibiting economic discrimination, our legal system insulates it from the reach of civil rights law. Our system allows easy circumvention of fair housing law when discrimination takes the form of financial requirements or if exclusion is attributed to protection of property interests. Such economic discrimination has been accorded a race-neutrality belied by the prevalence of hypersegregated Black urban ghettos. Courts protect commonplace assertions of racial privilege by designating the tendencies of middle-class whites to flee school and residential integration as de facto (and therefore irremediable) segregation. This protection of established racial and economic privilege is so embedded in our society that formal equality is rendered meaningless to poor minority Americans.[5]

To truly eradicate housing segregation, our society must examine and challenge the way our legal system reinforces two underlying assumptions: that white people have the privilege of escaping people of color, and that anyone who can afford to is entitled to abandon the urban poor. By casting economic discrimination as color-blind and as an unassailable right, American law ignores the symbiotic relationship between employment discrimination, urban poverty, and contemporary residential segregation. This relationship permits the illusion of separable societies.

The polarization of the privileged and the unprivileged in our society is reflected in the divergent demographics of South Central Los Angeles and Simi Valley in Ventura County. The population of

South Central Los Angeles is 52.8 percent African American and 41.9 percent Hispanic. The south central region of Los Angeles was once inhabited predominantly by African American working-class families employed in manufacturing plants located along a local railroad corridor. Today "those jobs have largely dried up, leaving the area with a negligible source of local employment."[6] The unemployment rate in the African American communities in Los Angeles is as high as 50 percent. Those who are able to leave these neighborhoods do; the number of Black people who live in the city of Los Angeles decreased between 1980 and 1990.

Simi Valley, in contrast, is a "garden spot with safe streets, good schools [and] a nice industrial base."[7] It has a population of approximately 100,000, many of whom left Los Angeles and its substantial population of people of color. Only 1.5 percent of the suburb's residents are African American. Suburban housing tends to be in the form of individually owned houses, whereas "two thirds of the families in South Central Los Angeles rent their small stucco bungalows, and they live there because they cannot afford to live anywhere else."[8] Despite state legislation requiring local governments to ensure that the housing needs of all income groups are met, California's suburban communities avoid setting up affordable housing programs by using techniques such as under-assessing low-income housing needs and enacting ordinances that restrict the supply of housing. But even though the residents of central Los Angeles cannot readily move to the suburbs, the suburbs come to them every day. Eighty-three percent of the Los Angeles police force live outside the city limits.

Despite rejecting Los Angeles as a place to live, a number of Simi Valley residents maintain weekday association with the city as commuters. Some of these commuters are Los Angeles police officers: the town has been described as a white, middle-class "bedroom community" for police. Suburbanites tend to see the police as a "thin blue line" or "bulwark against urban chaos and crime." Apparently, during working hours the police are driven by the attitude of revulsion felt by the privileged toward ghetto inhabitants; at night they rejoin the privileged in the suburbs. The police serve as contact points, forced to confine people who have deliberately been left behind in the chaos and who know they have little chance of escaping it.

The acquittal of the officers in the first Rodney King beating trial reflects this view of the police as a breakwater.

> Living just up the freeway and over the hills from Los Angeles, the jurors ended up viewing the four police officers as their own protection against the spread of inner-city crime . . . . The jurors feared "that if they punished these cops they would be less safe in their little community up there."[9]

Simi Valley and other suburban residents long ago surrendered Los Angeles to the perceived enemy and attempted to evade any responsibility to the city. But it was impossible to completely sever connections to Los Angeles because no suburb, particularly a "bedroom community" for urban employees, can cut its economic, cultural, and infrastructural ties to its urban center. A larger network of interdependency binds the residents of a metropolitan area, and of our nation as a whole. Suburban Americans "cannot escape responsibility for choosing the future of our metropolitan areas and the human relations that develop within them."[10] The connections retained by urban police officers peculiarly reinforce the sense of white entitlement to an area that is off limits to most people of color. To residents who come face to face with urban crime and poverty on the job, Simi Valley must seem a well-deserved home and resting place. Here, the besieged police can exercise the "earned" privilege of taking refuge from their work day battles with the unprivileged.

All over the United States, our cities are ringed by Ventura Counties, exclusive enclaves where middle-class people retreat in order to shut out urban problems. Americans have fled the cities in astonishing numbers. The 1992 presidential election was the first in which over 50 percent of the votes were cast by people who lived in the suburbs. Although there has been an increase in Black suburbanization compared to white suburbanization, relatively few Blacks reside in suburbs. Those that do live in predominantly Black suburbs.

Many suburban residents continue to derive their income from the cities they have abandoned, but more and more frequently their employers also forsake the cities. With this exodus, middle-class and business interest in the welfare of the city dries up. Consequently, resources are redirected to the locus of their perceived interest—the suburbs. The result is a regressive redistribution of the costs of having a society that includes poor people, by which city residents who are least able to pay bear the lion's share of the expenses of poverty.

Living Where You Want

There are places in America where you are not supposed to be if your skin is black or brown. Should an African American or Latino (particularly a young male) walk through the streets of certain suburbs, towns, or urban neighborhoods, he might notice that the inhabitants view his presence with suspicion, resentment, or worse. A person of color can be in danger in such areas, which are inexorably linked with violent attacks on people of color who happen to pass through. Infamous examples are Bensonhurst in Brooklyn, where sixteen-year-old Yusef Hawkins was murdered when he came to the area to look at a used car, and the Howard Beach section of Queens, where Michael Griffin was chased to his death by a gang of local residents. Although some perpetrators of racially motivated violence attribute their actions to security concerns, others openly admit that they believe their neighborhoods should be reserved for whites.

Nonwhite visitors are greeted with palpable hostility in white enclaves because the residents collectively establish and enforce an extralegal "right" to practice racial discrimination. Although statutes explicitly prohibit racial discrimination in most housing transactions, the extralegal right receives more respect and private enforcement than the actual housing discrimination laws. Neighborhood residents protect and implement this "right" to discriminate. Transgressions against this right are redressed rapidly through violence, while violations of the legal right against discrimination require bureaucracy, lawyers, or courts for enforcement. The false "right" arises from notions of entitlement and the primacy accorded property ownership in American legal and constitutional tradition. Some white Americans believe that property ownership carries with it entitlement to racial exclusivity—by earning enough money they acquire the privilege of residing "where they want." Other residents of white segregated neighborhoods explicitly believe that living where you want is a right or privilege incident to being born with white skin.

The continued existence of predominantly white or predominantly minority neighborhoods and suburbs that appear to defy fair housing law has been attributed by some analysts to the cumulative expression of individual choices. This cynical use of "consumer preference" attempts to disclaim government or societal responsibility for segregation. At the same time it falsely implies that freedom of choice works in a neutral manner. Free choice, however, is not available to all Americans. Generally, only white residents of segregated areas are able to actually exclude members of other races from residing in their communities. Although there is a growing movement of people of color who choose to live in predominantly black or brown neighborhoods, minority residents have traditionally been denied participation in shaping the configuration of their residential environments where there is any white interest in the area. Although some African Americans affirmatively choose Black neighborhoods, many Blacks who live in segregated middle-class neighborhoods would prefer more integration or may have originally moved to an integrated neighborhood that resegregated because of white flight.

The urban minority poor find themselves doubly abandoned due to the exercise of two forms of privilege. Because the privilege of living where one wishes is disbursed on the basis of income as well as race, middle-class Americans of color also attempt to relinquish the urban ghettos to the poor. Some move to middle-class Black neighborhoods, but many seek housing in predominantly white integrated communities in which the populations are healthier and the neighborhoods offer superior services, better schools, and more resources. Urban and suburban areas that are substandard, burdened by crime, environmental degradation, and wretched schools are more likely to house predominantly minority populations. Amenities that middle-class people take for granted, such as banks, supermarkets, and stores that provide basic goods and services, are scarce in low-income minority neighborhoods. Simply put, it is difficult to enjoy the benefits of a middle-class lifestyle in a poor minority neighborhood.

Indeed, if they wish to remain members of the middle class, Black residents are almost forced to leave urban inner city neighborhoods because the areas provide limited opportunity to earn a living legally. The staggering unemployment figures for inner-city neighborhoods reflect a vicious circle whereby the neighborhoods provide little work and the low-income populations are too poor to move closer to areas where work can be found. The scarcity of employment opportunity is coupled with rampant employment discrimination against African Americans. In the end, our inner cities are inhabited by people who have no means of leaving. If the choice of abandoning our inner cities was truly available to all Americans, our ghettos would surely become ghost towns.

Economic Privilege and Residential Access

Race plays a potent role in access to housing in America, but financial status is probably the primary factor in residential exclusion. The inability to pay the price of housing excludes prospective home-seekers across racial lines. But the fact that financial determinants can operate against white people as well as against Black people does not mean that economic discrimination is race-neutral.

Many Americans see nothing wrong with using economic status to distribute access to housing opportunities. Economic discrimination, however, enables our nation to preserve and continue widespread racial exclusivity in the composition of our communities. Although acknowledgment of the racial implications of economic privilege may be psychologically difficult, people who are concerned about integration and equal opportunity must consider the ramifications of economic privilege. When the protection of privilege is elevated above the goal of racial equality, the consequence is residential segregation. This segregation will not be limited to economically elite communities, because upper-middle-class behavior sets a standard by which success is measured. Therefore, high-income whites cannot live in segregated areas and expect lower-income whites to abstain from using their racial privilege in similar ways.

Our society uses economic privilege as a means of controlling access to good neighborhoods. Because America is a democracy that promises equality of opportunity, it would be unfair to arbitrarily deny people the prospect of residing in a decent environment. Thus, in order to justify the exclusion of the poor from safe areas with access to public services and good schools, income is used as a measure of worthiness. Economic privilege seems less inequitable if we pretend that it is distributed on the basis of merit.

The 1980s saw a resurgence in blaming poor people for their want of advantage. Being unprivileged was no longer ascribed to misfortune or racism, it became a matter of just desserts. Under this line of reasoning, people who live in substandard areas or who are destitute are unprivileged because of their own decisions. The poor "choose" to drop out of school, to become teenage mothers, to apply for welfare; the unemployed are "determined" not to work. This attitude toward the unprivileged is rooted in the American mythology that any person, through her own will and effort, can work her way out of poverty. Such dogma neutralizes the unfairness of privilege by casting it not as something granted selectively, but as something obtainable by all.

If privilege can be achieved, then lack of privilege is attributable to individual choice; in other words, the only thing preventing the poor from gaining privilege is their own lack of ambition or diligence. Because most people obtain their financial success through employment and do not see themselves as being unfairly advantaged, economic privilege is viewed as "earned." Since we work hard to obtain financial status rather than simply being lucky enough to inherit it as some form of birthright, economic privilege does not appear arbitrary or gratuitous. In fact, many Americans take it for granted that wealth should provide distance from poverty and the poor; they even see it as a reward and incentive for hard work. Such attitudes are blind to the fact that many of the poor work hard, yet are not rewarded with privilege.[11] A disproportionate number of minority Americans are among the working poor or involuntarily unemployed who lack privilege. Our opinions about poor people sentence those who are unable to work, due to no fault of their own, to a world with few options and limited futures. A large number of the poor are children who are unable to "earn" the privilege of living in middle-class neighborhoods. Children in poor and minority areas are often accorded mediocre or substandard educations, which further impair their ability to compete for the type of work that could reward them with access to middle-class privilege. In the end, economic privilege distributes benefits and privilege capriciously, because, despite hard work, willingness to work, or inability to work, poor minorities are excluded from the opportunity to earn the financial status that provides an escape to areas available to the more privileged. For many people poverty results from structural deficiencies more than from their individual failings. Economic privilege is not uniformly disseminated on the basis of merit and is, at best, an unjust and inadequate rationale for the segregation of the poor. It also serves as a mask to conceal unlawful exclusion for purposes of preserving racial privilege.

Although we may recognize that when the poor are denied access to middle- and upper-class neighborhoods, economic privilege perpetuates racial segregation, our courts fail to acknowledge the legal wrong. The courts give economic status such primacy that considerations of wealth actually insulate otherwise prohibited housing discrimination from legal scrutiny. These general notions of wealth and earned privilege are replicated and prevail, even in the administration of our fair housing laws.

Protecting Privilege

The idea that race and money entitle people to the privilege of residential choice and the actual prerogative to exclude those who are not similarly privileged is a powerful influence in our society. Concepts of privilege are so firmly held as to effectively constitute a "right" in the minds of many American property owners. Most frequently, courts protect the "right" to engage in racial discrimination as an unspoken corollary of the right to discriminate on the basis of income. Courts also reinforce popular notions of an extralegal "right" to discriminate on the basis of race by recognizing residential segregation as a legal impediment to judicial intervention in school desegregation cases.

The jurisprudence of housing discrimination generally rejects protection of the poor as a group, and there is no fundamental right to housing under federal constitutional analysis. A series of U.S.

Supreme Court cases, decided primarily in the 1970s, refused to recognize poverty as a suspect classification or to find that legislation
discriminating against the poor is subject to strict judicial scrutiny.

State and local legislation directed at excluding the poor is a barrier to the effective enforcement of federal civil rights law. Economic
rationales, such as keeping property taxes low, provide a very convenient wrapper for concealing impermissible discrimination. John
Calmore describes the predictable outcome of judicial deference to
wealth-determined distinctions:

> Although in absolute numbers there are more white poor than
> Black poor, Blacks carry a disproportionate burden of poverty,
> and thus many times their claims for substantive distributive
> justice are essentially race claims. Often, what begins as a claim
> concerning the effects of racial discrimination gets transformed
> in constitutional analysis into a complaint not of racial but eco-
> nomic injustice and then denied in the reformulated terms.[12]

When our courts refuse to recognize economic class as a suspect category they protect legally prohibited racial discrimination, allowing
those who discriminate to frustrate civil rights goals and block some
of the limited steps American society has taken to eradicate poverty.

Opposition to the placement of subsidized housing in middle-
class neighborhoods illustrates the clash of economic privilege and
racial justice. Although a handful of federal programs have recognized the need for low-income housing and provided funding, local
resistance often thwarts their implementation. Opponents of low-
income housing attempt to block it by protesting that the development will interfere with their property values. Courts consistently
find preservation of this economic privilege more compelling than
protecting the poor from exclusion. Such cases ignore the tendency
of the American public to equate poverty with minority races. When

legislators are able to label a concern economic, examination of the law's racial impact is diverted and discriminatory legislation is permitted to escape exacting scrutiny. This dynamic is illustrated by *James v. Valtierra*,[13] in which the U.S. Supreme Court denied an equal protection challenge to a provision of the California State Constitution. This provision, enacted through the voter referendum process, required voter approval of low-rent housing projects. Although the provision singles out housing for the poor for electoral approval, and subjects no other type of development to this requirement, the Court found the provision to embody democratic ideals, writing,

> This procedure ensures that all the people of a community will have a voice in a decision which may lead to large expenditures of local governmental funds for increased public services and to lower tax revenues. It gives them a voice in decisions that will affect the future development of their own community. This procedure for democratic decisionmaking does not violate the constitutional command that no State shall deny to any person "the equal protection of the laws."[14]

James v. Valtierra epitomizes the exclusionary force of economic privilege. A popularly perceived entitlement to exclude the poor is transformed into a constitutional right. Although property owners feel that their ownership entitles them to many "rights" to limit inimical uses of neighboring property, subsidized housing is the only residential land use decision accorded the status of necessitating individual input from the local inhabitants. The *James* decision characterizes the right to exclude as the embodiment of democratic principles. The poor are forever excluded from the community without ever having a chance to participate in the democratic process that banishes them. The Court refused to examine the racial implications of California's constitutional provision, stating that it was "seemingly neutral on its face."[15]

Court decisions in cases brought under the Fair Housing Act have not protected the poor as a class from discrimination any more effectively than have equal protection decisions. In *Boyd v. Lefrak Org.*, prospective renters challenged as racially discriminatory the income requirements imposed by a management company that was already subject to a consent decree from a previous pattern and practice suit under the Fair Housing Act.[16] The landlord required that applicants have a weekly *net* income (deducting all taxes, fixed obligations, and debts) that was at least 90 percent of the monthly rental (the 90 percent rule), or to have a guarantor whose weekly net income was 110 percent of the monthly rental. Expert testimony at trial indicated that the income requirements excluded 92.5 percent of local Black and Puerto Rican households, and that white household eligibility would be four times as great as that of Black households and ten times as great of as that of Puerto Rican households. The district court found that the defendant's income criteria violated the Fair Housing Act due to a "disproportionately high racially discriminatory impact" and that the defendant did not establish a business necessity or other non-racial grounds for the rule.[17] In reversing the judgment of the district court, the circuit court wrote,

> While blacks and Puerto Ricans do not have the same access to Lefrak apartments as do whites, the reason for this inequality is not racial discrimination but rather the disparity in economic level among these groups. . . . A businessman's differential treatment of different economic groups is not necessarily racial discrimination and is not made so because minorities are statistically overrepresented in poorer economic groups. The fact that differentiation in eligibility rates for defendants' apartments is

correlated with race proves merely that minorities tend to be poorer than is the general population.[18]

The court noted that although a disparate impact analysis might be appropriate in a challenge to state action, it could ignore the racially exclusionary results of the defendant's policy because the policy applied uniform economic criteria to whites and minorities. The majority in *Boyd* framed the issue as the ability of a landlord to use economic factors to judge prospective tenants. An alternative characterization of the issues presented could focus on the exclusionary effects of the landlord's economic criteria, to determine if they were designed to evade prohibitions against racial discrimination. The opinion instead accords the income requirements the presumption of neutrality, while failing to examine their contextual ramifications. The court ignored the fact that the 90 percent rule was devised by a management company that was subject to a consent decree for previous violations of the Fair Housing Act. These prior violations might have provided evidence that the requirements were intended to result in prohibited racial exclusion.

In *Boyd*, the right to engage in economic discrimination was more palpable in the eyes of the majority than the racial discrimination it advanced. The plaintiffs had a "right" to not be discriminated against on the basis of race, but were not protected against economic discrimination. Again, a court refused to even examine whether racial discrimination occurred because the defendant could present a theory of economic discrimination.

A state statute that the California courts have held to prohibit arbitrary discrimination in housing, California's Unruh Civil Rights Act,[19] has been limited judicially to exclude discrimination based on poverty. In *Harris v. Capital Growth Investors XIV*,[20] the California Supreme Court refused to remedy economic exclusion that caused prohibited discriminatory impact, even when the insubstantial nature of the economic rationale indicated other noneconomic motives. Income requirements that went beyond those necessary to protect the economic interests of a landlord were upheld even though these requirements disproportionately excluded female-headed households from the pool of applicants to whom the defendants would rent units. Policies that limit the housing available to female-headed households also exclude a disproportionately high percentage of minorities.

The court refused to examine the defendant's policy because it was applicable to all applicants regardless of race, color, sex, or religion. The justices found it unimportant that applying the policy to all people would result in excluding members of statutorily protected groups significantly more than it would exclude households headed by white males. Because the defendant cited economic status as the basis of the exclusion, the court could shift its focus to the financial ramifications of the policy. When the balance focused on economic interests, protecting privilege was accorded more importance than the total exclusion of low-income people, even those who in fact could pay market rate for the housing. Economic interest again served as a trump card, overriding all other considerations. The *Harris* court explicitly granted considerations of wealth primacy over actual discriminatory impact, even when the biased act was not necessary to protect financial interests.

Thus, the concept of economic privilege is used to justify and sustain the de facto residential segregation of the poor, and, thereby, of many people of color. It has resulted in the concentration of low-income minorities in center-city neighborhoods throughout the United States. Because our society believes that anyone who can afford to live in an affluent suburb is entitled to leave the city and its problems, and since the route to privilege can be achieved by some minorities, it is argued that the existence of urban ghettos is attributable to economic factors rather than to racial discrimination. It is clear, however, that a person of color is much more likely to be excluded from the prospect of earning enough money to "buy" the privilege of escaping to the suburbs, and that income simply reinforces race as a means of keeping Blacks in the inner city. Furthermore, an African American and a white American with identical educational and financial backgrounds do not have an identical range of housing choices or employment opportunities.[21]

Two problems accompany the great magnitude of judicial deference to economic privilege. One problem is that the deference allows prohibited residential racial discrimination to occur as long as a housing provider can attribute exclusion to economic factors. The second problem with the primacy of economic privilege is that it is distributed unjustly. Economic privilege is not allocated to all who might merit it and is still disproportionately unavailable to African Americans.

The second prong of privilege is white racial privilege. White privilege involves advantages and options that are available merely because one is white. A white person need not be a bigot to benefit from racial privilege; simply having white skin means having access to neighborhoods and jobs that are closed to people of color. Living in such neighborhoods is not, for every resident, an assertion of racial hostility, but many of these areas are sought out by whites because the environment is inhospitable to minorities.

Racial privilege is manifest in the divergent presumptions and perceptions accorded to individuals on the basis of their race. The influence of race as a barrier to better neighborhoods is discounted because the law no longer countenances explicit racial barriers in housing opportunities; therefore the obstacles to escaping ghetto neighborhoods are seen as economic and self-imposed.

Racial privilege tends to be advanced by whites who can work in concert as a community to reinforce exclusion. This is the form of privilege asserted by numerous ethnic groups of European origin who assert that they have the right to maintain segregated enclaves in order to preserve their ethnic or religious identity. Although individuals who are caught discriminating against other identified individuals are subject to state sanction, minorities are kept out of white neighborhoods by strategies more complex than individual denials of housing. Punishable acts of discrimination are the exception, so minorities are excluded with legal impunity.

The facts and holding of *City of Memphis v. Greene*[22] present an example of this dynamic. In *Greene*, white residents of Hein Park, a Memphis community bordered to the north by a predominantly Black area, requested the city to close a street (West Drive) that served as an artery between the two neighborhoods, ostensibly to reduce traffic and increase safety in Hein Park. The closure would be effectuated by the city's selling a twenty-five foot strip that ran across West Drive to the northernmost property owners in the white area. Residents of the African American community to the north of Hein Park challenged the sale under the U.S. Constitution and 42 U.S.C. §§ 1982 and 1983.

The United States Supreme Court upheld the closing despite sixth circuit findings that evidence presented to the district court showed the closing would benefit a white neighborhood and would adversely affect Blacks, and that the "barrier was to be erected precisely at the point of separation of these neighborhoods and would undoubtedly have the effect of limiting contact between them."[23] Instead, the Supreme Court found that

> the critical facts established by the record are these: The city's decision to close West Drive was motivated by its interest in protecting the safety and tranquility of a residential neighborhood. . . . The city has conferred a benefit on white property owners but there is no reason to believe that it would refuse to confer a comparable benefit on black property owners. The closing has not affected the value of property owned by black

citizens, but it has caused some slight inconvenience to black motorists.[24]

The Supreme Court majority in *Greene* held that the closing was for traffic safety purposes, ignoring the fact that the closing of West Drive was the only time the city of Memphis had ever closed a street for traffic control purposes. Although the city and the Supreme Court majority coated the actions of the Hein Park residents with a veneer of neutrality, the motives behind the decision to close West Drive remain apparent. As the dissent in *Greene* noted, "Respondents are being sent a clear, though sophisticated message that because of their race they are to stay out of the all-white enclave of Hein Park and should instead take the long way around in reaching their destinations to the south."[25] *Greene* provided judicial support and legal enforcement for an extralegal white "right" to exclude minorities, even though such a "right" could not be explicitly acknowledged by a court.

Recent cases examining school desegregation and housing discrimination demonstrate that our highest courts are blind to racial segregation that can be attributed to economic privilege. In *Board of Educ. of Okla. City Pub. Sch. v. Dowell*, the board argued that segregation in its schools was due to private decision making and economics that created residential segregation.[26] The U.S. Supreme Court picked up this theme, embracing without question a right to use financial privilege to resegregate. Again, in *Freeman v. Pitts*,[27] the U.S. Supreme Court lent its imprimatur to racial segregation based on individual privilege and choice. The Court recognized as inevitable, and thus sanctioned, residential segregation based on the preferences of whites:

> The effect of changing residential patterns on the racial composition of schools though not always fortunate is somewhat predictable. Studies show a high correlation between residential

segregation and school segregation. . . . The District Court in
this case heard evidence tending to show that racially stable
neighborhoods are not likely to emerge because whites prefer a
racial mix of 80% white and 20% black, while blacks prefer a
50% – 50% mix. Where resegregation is a product not of state
action but of private choices, it does not have constitutional
implications. . . . Residential housing choices and their atten-
dant effects on the racial composition of schools, present an
ever-changing pattern, one difficult to address through judicial
remedies.[28]

Thus, Justice Kennedy decreed that when racial isolation is of societal proportions but results from the free market and individual
choice, the Court should not intervene. Neither *Dowell* nor *Freeman*
addressed the issue of which individuals get a chance to actively participate in the market and to exercise choice. The law can absolve
itself from further inquiry if a judge affixes the de facto label, even in
cases where the court explicitly recognizes that segregation is occur-
ring. Our courts' refusal to recognize the impact of segregation based
on individual choice implicates the legal system as a force that sustains segregation. Even in the absence of de jure segregation, America
still finds residential and educational segregation intractable. Racial
separation will remain imbedded in our system because it relies on
the unassailable concept of economic privilege to obscure deliberate
segregation.

The Myth of Economic Choice and the Promise of Equality

As suburban America feels increasingly insecure about preserving its
status and property, attempts to isolate the middle class from the
unprivileged have increased accordingly. Tax revolts, suburban office
parks, concrete traffic barriers, and walled private neighborhoods
and towns are all evidence of a desire to limit contact with the less

privileged. The tenet that one of the perquisites of money is to be able to isolate oneself from the unprivileged sustains a societal separation that is illusory and incendiary. Although the urge to reject the urban ghetto is real, the privileged can only pretend to sequester themselves from contact and connection with the unprivileged. The disintegration of the urban center city contributes to the deterioration of the ethical and physical quality of life in society as a whole. Attempts to maintain the illusion that poverty is not a problem for those better off simply magnify the glaring differences between the lives of the rich and poor and ensure that the inevitable contact of the polarized segments of our society will be explosive.

It is time for our law to recognize that economic discrimination creates a sub rosa system of extralegal discriminatory "rights" that directly conflict with our express legal norms prohibiting discrimination. The fact that discrimination on the basis of race in housing transactions is no longer legal does not, by itself, create equal access to communities like Simi Valley. As long as there is no real chance for a family in inner-city Los Angeles to choose to move to Ventura County, we cannot honestly say that our society provides equal opportunity at any level. No one believes that the education at a public school in South Central Los Angeles is equal to the education offered at a public school in Simi Valley. Were there truly equal opportunity, many of the families of South Central Los Angeles would move to areas where they could send their kids to the schools that really provide a chance for the better life. These families do not remain in blighted neighborhoods from a lack of desire for better futures for their children. They simply have little opportunity to choose where they live.

It is also time for the law to stop shielding racial discrimination by labeling it "economic choice." Left to our own devices we Americans make the wrong choices—choices based on obtaining or maintaining privilege—with little thought to the corresponding exclusion of the least fortunate of the American community. A look at the demographics of housing in the United States reveals that many in our nation still choose residential segregation and, by doing so, deny choice to those who would opt for integration. The comparison between life in the neighborhoods of South Central Los Angeles and life for Ventura County residents illustrates that the choice to discriminate imposes burdens on the rest of society.

It is clear that America has never firmly resolved to eradicate residential racial segregation. Thirty years ago Judge Loren Miller wrote, "Resistance [to fair housing laws] will persist as long as there is hope that 'white' communities can be maintained at all price levels; it will diminish when the householder who fears Negro occupancy is convinced that he can run but cannot hide from Negro neighbors."[29] But until society genuinely works toward eliminating separate communities for Black and white Americans, our society will live in constant conflict. The conflict will arise both from our failure to uphold our laws that promise fairness in access and from the resentment of those excluded. The isolation of minority Americans is a barrier to our country's social and economic progress. Unless we move forward in eliminating segregation by recognizing how it is advanced by our protection of economic privilege, we are destined to remain standing still.

We cannot sequester the poor out of existence and we cannot maintain impermeable barriers between the different segments of society without defying basic principles of liberty and equal protection. If our society pretends that its component communities are separate and hostile spheres, the unavoidable interaction will be between angry and fearful factions, as demonstrated in the police beating of Rodney King, the acquittal of the officers, and the upheaval that followed.

As long as the poor do not have any realistic chance of escaping poverty or leaving the ghetto, they are pinioned to the bottom of society by concepts of privilege that have arbitrarily excluded them from a better life. Although those of us with options that allow us to live where we choose may be more fortunate than meritorious, we erect insurmountable barriers between ourselves and the poor in order to maintain our privileged positions. However, even though the promise of equal access is far from being kept, it has been made and renewed. The lesson our society must learn from the uprising that followed the Simi Valley acquittals is that those to whom the pledge of equality was made have not forgotten America's promises and refuse to allow themselves to be forgotten.

Chapter 4

Adrienne D. Davis and
Stephanie M. Wildman

Privilege and the Media
Treatment of Sex and Race
in the Hill-Thomas Hearings
Create a Legacy of Doubt

Clarence Thomas has been sworn in as the 106th Supreme Court justice. He is the second African American justice. After weeks of televised confirmation hearings, extensive public debate among citizens
and in the media, and the final Senate vote, questions still remain
whether justice has been served.

Television added a different dimension to the process, which
became a human drama when Professor Anita Hill's sexual harassment claim and Thomas's denial were aired. The nation watched mes-
merized, waiting for a Perry Mason to rise and announce who had

An earlier version of this chapter appeared as Adrienne D. Davis and Stephanie
M.Wildman, *The Legacy of Doubt: Treatment of Sex and Race in the Hill-Thomas
Hearings*, 65 SO. CAL. L. REV. 1367 (1992), copyright © 1992 by Adrienne D. Davis
and Stephanie M. Wildman. Reprinted with permission.

lied, but no Perry Mason appeared. We have only ourselves to assess credibility and to record history. The complex role of the media in supporting systems of privilege is exemplified in these events.

Even since the confirmation vote, the controversy over who told the truth has not been put to rest. Newspaper op-ed pieces, an episode of a popular prime-time television show, *Designing Women*, and a *People* magazine cover story only begin to illustrate the extent to which these events have touched a national nerve.

Clarence Thomas ascended the bench with a legacy of doubt. There were doubts as to whether his qualifications merited confirmation and doubts about his character because of sexual harassment allegations and implications of dishonesty. By the end of the confirmation process the doubts had broadened beyond Thomas himself. Doubts remain as to whether those who have not experienced sexual harassment want to understand it. Depictions of women in society as sexually accessible objects disable efforts of those who do want to understand. Doubts remain as to whether the privileging and disempowering dynamics of race, experienced by each member of society, will ever be fathomed. The presence of an implicitly masculine gender in the symbol race confounds any effort to identify racism, white supremacy, and the dynamics of race. Doubts remain as to whether these events, as portrayed for popular consumption, distort even further the issues of racism, sexism, and decision making in this country. And finally, these doubts implicate the Senate's capacity as a male institution to effectively represent all Americans.

Sexual Harassment, Female Commodification, and Credibility

Recent legal scholarship has suggested that perceptions of women and men may differ regarding sexual harassment.[1] Abundant evidence indicated that sexual harassment was regarded as unimportant by the Senate in the events leading up to the hearings concerning Anita Hill's charges. Her statement had been submitted to the full

Senate Judiciary Committee on September 23, 1991,[2] and the committee members evidently had no plan to make the allegations known to their colleagues.[3] Only when National Public Radio correspondent Nina Totenberg aired the complaint[4] and *Newsday* ran the story[5] did a furor begin, culminating in demands that the committee regard these charges as a serious obstacle to confirmation. After the public outpouring indicated that many constituents regarded a complaint of sexual harassment as serious, the Senate did delay the confirmation vote on Thomas and agreed to further investigate the allegations. The public outcry dragged the senators from the position of white male privilege that had allowed them to ignore the charges.

In spite of the senators' public protestations to the contrary, a dismissive attitude toward sexual harassment pervaded comments made by senators as well as the press. Among the most egregious was Senator Alan Simpson's statement that during the course of the hearings Hill would experience "real harassment," not just sexual harassment.[6] This comment suggested that at least one senator on the Judiciary Committee considered sexual harassment a marginal issue at best. The failure of the Senate to call expert witnesses on sexual harassment in order to inform themselves and to place the issue in its legal and social context further evidenced the peripheral status accorded the allegations.

The press gave only brief coverage to one astonishing example of the lack of importance with which senators viewed sexual harassment. Wanda Baucus, the wife of Senator Max Baucus, told the press that she telephoned many senators personally during the hearings. She herself had been harassed as a guest at Senate social functions and as a working woman. She thought that she could help the senators learn about sexual harassment. She found that the problem was not their lack of awareness of sexual harassment:

> As I was calling various members of the Senate on both sides of
> the aisle last week, they were telling me things that made me fall

off my chair. When I telephoned one of the people on the Democratic side over the weekend, who had already planned to and did vote for the nomination, he said, "Oh yes, I knew these things go on," somewhat with surprised amusement.[7]

Evidently the problem was not lack of knowledge, but lack of understanding or caring.

Baucus's story demonstrates that sexual harassment and ignorance regarding its gravity are pervasive and not limited to the workplace, although the occurrence of harassment there is particularly insidious. Sexual harassment is rooted in the exploitation of women that occurs in every aspect of our society. Many, if not most, of the advertisements on national television that interrupted the Senate Hearings featured women portrayed as sexual objects.[8] The national image of women as accessible to men for sex is a powerful stereotype that commodifies and harms women.[9] Women are probably the most widely used marketing tool in the advertising industry: young, thin, unwrinkled, mostly white women sell everything from beer to food to cars to the value of exercise. They do not even need to speak: the idea implicitly conveyed is that if you buy this product, this woman, or one like her, will be attracted to you, as she is to the man in the ad.

Women are a commodity like any other, except that they do not cost anything. In one beer commercial a group of men say, "It just doesn't get any better than this." They then find a crate of lobster in the river, the Swedish bikini team lands in the area and starts gyrating, and, finally, the beer arrives. Although they rated as more important than the lobsters, women have become the unspoken yet assumed reward, the unmentioned "added value" of the product.

Even within the workplace—perhaps especially within the workplace—part of the job that women as a group perform is to add a touch of femininity and decoration. Women are regularly evaluated on how attractive they are in addition to how well they perform. Many women internalize this standard and think that the ideal "woman" must be "feminine" as defined by men. The billions of dollars women spend every year on makeup, clothes, and special youth creams cannot be because they are born wanting to look like some idealized image of beauty. At some point these women come to understand that they are viewed as commodities. The value of women as commodities is derived from a market of desirability as defined by men. This valuation might be criticized for many reasons, including that it denies women's self-determination, it privileges men's definition of women, and it privileges heterosexism. In other words, you can choose not to play, but if you are going to play, you might as well win.

It is against this stereotype of male valuation and sexual availability that any woman will be measured when she complains of sexual harassment. Although it is false, the (usually) unspoken message is that only a "desirable" woman will be harassed.[10] Ironically, as women seek to make themselves desirable to men, they are blamed for male response. This "blame the victim" attitude suggests that somehow the woman "asked for it," as if anyone would wish to be sexually harassed. Yet the stereotype of women as sexually available leads to the perception that women wish for this kind of attention. For some, this image was enough to make them discredit Hill's testimony. The term "erotomania" was used to describe women's desire for sexual involvement with men in powerful positions. Virginia Lamp Thomas, Clarence Thomas's wife, offered as her explanation that Hill "was probably . . . in love with my husband."[11]

Like many viewers, we found Hill's testimony credible. Those who did question her credibility repeatedly asked why she had not come forward sooner, why she moved with Thomas from the Department of Education to the EEOC, and why she had maintained her connections to Thomas by phone calls. We found Hill's behavior absolutely consistent with her charge of sexual harassment. First, Hill did not initiate the contact with the Senate Judiciary Committee. In addition, it would be unreasonable to have expected Hill to jeopardize her career by alienating Thomas after leaving his employ. In this era of networking, the importance of maintaining connection with someone who might be called as a reference cannot be minimized. It is not a coincidence that she waited to speak until after she had a tenured teaching position, which should make her job, at least, secure, although some press reports suggested that the University of Oklahoma was pressured to reexamine her tenure.

The attack on Hill's credibility relating to sexual harassment repeated a patriarchal cycle of devaluing women. Her treatment during the confirmation process more closely approximated "lynching" than the gentle treatment Thomas received.[12] Comparing gender to race discrimination is troubling, because such comparisons tend to minimize the seriousness of race discrimination and also render invisible the experience of women of color, who cannot divide themselves and their experiences into a race part and a gender part. Yet the comparison is a useful one, because it serves to illustrate the seriousness of sex discrimination. "[O]ne is struck by certain parallels between Hill's treatment by the male establishment and blacks' treatment by white communities in the Old South."[13]

Hill's treatment by the Senate Judiciary Committee suggested that she occupied an unprotected space in today's society, as did Blacks in the old South, where no white person would question another white's treatment of his slaves. Men on the Judiciary Committee were unwilling to ask Thomas probing questions, and when Hill testified, her allegations were not taken seriously. Senators sought to dismiss her as delusional or engaged in fantasy. Thus we see another similarity to the Old South, where during slavery testimony by Blacks against whites was prohibited and, even after Reconstruction, remained a rare event.

> Lynchings were public events held for the purpose of delivering a message of intimidation to other blacks, promising that any explicit or implicit challenge or affront to a white person by a black person would result in the most extreme punishment. . . The message was clear: If Hill, a conservative, religious law professor telling a credible story of sexual harassment, could be dismissed out of hand, what recourse would any other women have?[14]

However, one of the lessons from this confirmation process is that women's reaction may not conform to expectations. As more women become conscious that the treatment they have regularly endured is harassment and is illegal, they will come forward.

Making the analogy between Hill's treatment and the treatment of Blacks in the Old South emphasizes the continuing force of patriarchy in American society. The behavior of the male Senate Judiciary Committee and Clarence Thomas paralleled the role of white plantation owners.[15] Thus maleness, regardless of race, entitles one to some of the benefits of patriarchy. Thomas was thus legitimated by being "one of the boys," whose possible taste for pornography was placed in a protected zone of privacy and whose workplace conduct was not seriously questioned. This legitimation of Thomas's male privilege was made even more complex by his own use of race, which emphasized his Blackness.

Gendering the Symbol "Race" and the Invisibility of Racism

A series of symbols mediated the public collective understanding of the Thomas confirmation hearings. In modern society, symbols increasingly mediate relationships in a variety of ways, from how people learn history to how they purchase commodities. Symbols provide indicators for historians of the "essence" of historical eras, the main images of words, pictures, and sounds that people welcomed (or rejected) in their lives. Symbols have also become more prevalent through American culture's increased reliance on such visual media as magazines and, particularly, television. Manufacturers of products hire ad agencies to create that snappy, product-invoking image that will be ingrained in the minds of the buying public. Symbols represent efforts to render understandable a complex world and to synthesize variant ideas and metaphors operating at multiple levels into a single, graspable entity.

To the extent that symbols filter understanding of events and, in particular, affect the way history will record them, the ability to share in their creation and presentation is paramount to constructing reality. When Clarence Thomas was first nominated, race became a prime symbol that served as a synthesis of questions over President Bush's motivations in nominating Thomas, his qualifications, affirmative action, and his background.

Race as a symbol appeared in fora as diverse as popular comedy shows, political cartoons, news coverage, and intellectual debate. From the beginning, Thomas controlled this symbol of race. He was the object, the referent of the symbol "Black." But unlike most objects, the press and the Bush administration gave him substantial power to define himself and the symbolic value of his signifier. The manipulation of the symbol was amazing: It was formally discounted, and yet the continued references to its absence made attention focus on it all the more. Race as constructed by Thomas became a symbol of making it on one's own, of searing poverty turned to economic privilege, of self-reliance over handouts. He attempted to depict as minimal any benefits of racial preferences he had received.

The symbolic value of race was temporarily replaced with that of gender when Anita Hill alleged she had been sexually harassed while on Thomas's staff. Women rallied to Hill's support because of the powerful symbol of sexual abuse, familiar to many women. At this point those seeking to discredit Hill transformed the image of gender oppression by sexual abuse into one of unrestrained sexuality. These two images, gender oppression and sexuality, were vying for primacy when Thomas reintroduced the symbol of race, which then became the axis around which all subsequent discourse revolved.

Thomas, a firm *dis*believer in the use of race as an excuse for one's behavior or as a reason for acting affirmatively to increase representation of underrepresented groups,[16] invoked race with a vengeance against the Senate Judiciary Committee. In claiming he was the victim of a high-tech lynching, Thomas claimed he was being accused because he was African American.

Consider the many valid reasons for which the senators should have called Thomas to account for his conduct: Hill's charges were supported by four different witnesses; the charges she brought would have exposed not only his character (as if that would not be enough), but also his lack of respect for the rule of law; and if true the charges would have demonstrated that he had perjured himself. Thomas's invocation of race at this point in the confirmation process was truly ironic. His use of race in these hearings rested on the implicit assertion that he was called to answer Hill's charges by virtue of the fact that he was an African American. Yet his accuser was also African American. The inconsistent treatment of the symbol "Black" as applied to Hill and Thomas revealed that the symbol was gendered. In this struggle, the symbol "Black" equaled male.

By saying he was being lynched, Thomas implicitly claimed he would have been treated differently (better?) if he had been white. Yet senators treated him quite well, deferring to his demands and tirades. No one suggested he was misusing race. No one pointed out that to do as he had suggested, let the whole matter go, would fit an equally heinous and embarrassing racial paradigm, that of ignoring the claims of sexual abuse brought by African American women. Instead, Thomas declared that suddenly his Senate friends were out to get him and that the white people he had claimed would respect hard work and self-reliance were treating him as if he were—Black?

Thus, in Thomas's manipulation of the symbol of race, Anita Hill became, somehow, "de-raced" and partially erased. For Thomas to have confronted the fact that his accuser was Black would have confused the racial point he was trying to make. Instead, in a stunning sleight of hand, he managed to convince all involved, including the Senate, that white racism, rather than a Black woman, had accused him of harassment. Thus, race became something Hill did not have. In an ironic twist of fate she became "Yale-educated female law professor" to Thomas's "lynched Black man." She became a part of the white racist conspiracy that Thomas asserted was after him. He had gained exclusive control over the content of the symbol "race," giving it a gender that allowed Hill no place within it, rendering her race invisible.

Patricia Williams has commented on this modern inclination to present issues of race as invisible. She told the story of her late godmother's bedroom, which she had cleared of furniture in order to paint. Even empty, the memories in the room had come flooding back to her; "the shape of the emptiness" confronting her each time she was about to enter:

> The power of that room, I have thought since, is very like the power of racism as status quo: it is deep, angry, eradicated from view, but strong enough to make everyone who enters the room walk around the bed that isn't there, avoiding the phantom as they did the substance, for fear of bodily harm. They do not even know they are avoiding; they defer to the unseen shapes of things with subtle responsiveness, guided by an impulsive awareness of nothingness, and the deep knowledge and denial of witchcraft at work.[17]

Williams's powerful description of racism as the phantom affecting everyone in society explains much about the Thomas hearing dynamic. The rendering invisible of Anita Hill's race, its exclusion from a discussion of her sexual harassment charge, meant racism/white supremacy was not discussed, except on Clarence Thomas's terms. Hill made her charge as an African-American woman in a society dominated by white male values. The erasure of her race allowed racism to act as a phantom once again.

The senators tried to avoid looking racist by refusing to ask Thomas any hard questions, and in doing so deferred to the "unseen shape" of racism. Yet by deferring, they fostered racism and its companion in America, white supremacy. The avoidance of race, the failure to talk about it or acknowledge its role in history, maintains and perpetuates racism/white supremacy. By avoiding race, we never have to confront the implications of change, and we default to the status quo that makes whiteness privileged. Failing to talk about race forces racism off limits, but it does not make either go away. Like people avoiding the phantom furniture in Williams's godmother's bedroom, we tiptoe around the dynamic of racism, keeping it intact.

Williams reported a chilling example of this denial of race in her own experience. She, a Black woman, was barred from a Benetton's store at Christmastime by a white clerk who refused to activate the buzzer that admitted shoppers. When she described this outrageous example of racism in a law review article, the editors edited out all reference to her race. When she retold this tale of law school editing, as showing the need to talk about race and to engage in affirmative action, her speech was reported as being *against* affirmative action. And finally, when another law professor discussed these events in class, a rumor started that Williams had made up the story about her exclusion from Benetton's.[18]

Thus her complaint about racism, exclusion from the store, was first distorted and then relegated by the white audience to the realm of fantasy, the ultimate denial of the presence of racism. The senators accused Anita Hill of fantasy, denoting a similar attempt to deny the possible existence of discriminatory behavior. Is the fate of Black women who tell stories of racism and sexism, like Williams and Hill, that they will not be believed?

An Example of the Treatment of Race and Sex in Popular Culture

Because of the primacy of symbols, political events enter mass consciousness by their depiction in popular culture. By this use of symbols, society attempts to understand events in a comfortable way. Symbols gain potency in the context of their depictions in popular culture. The intersections between life, art, and politics, and how the first is influenced by the latter two, have become more clear in the post-Thomas confirmation era.

The popularization of the hearings, indeed of Thomas himself, by television broadcast marked a new era for the Supreme Court and the legal system.[19] Television was a powerful force during the confirmation hearings, giving content to the pervasive symbols of race and sex. It is appropriate to consider the post hoc treatment of the Thomas confirmation by that mainstay of popular television, the half-hour prime time situation comedy.

CBS's *Designing Women* dedicated an episode to "The Strange Case of Clarence and Anita."[20] This broadcast signified a peculiar intersection between serious politics and popular art, embedded within a half-hour show with a laugh track. The themes debated in the show reflected the battle of symbols—gender oppression versus unrestrained sexuality—and the struggle over the gender of race disputed during the hearing.

The loose plot of the show operated on several levels. At the most basic level, the characters (five white women and one African American man) argued about the Hill-Thomas hearings, reducing the debate to an argument over whether "he did it" or "she lied."[21] At another level, the female characters joked with the male character about their own harassment of him as their employee. On still another plane, two of the characters (the progressive white females who believed Hill) appeared in a stage version of *Whatever Happened to Baby Jane?* Finally, these diverse themes merged in the final scene, in which the characters reconvened at a pajama party to reflect on the day's events.

The characters' debates over the credibility of Thomas and Hill strikingly echoed the actual discussions that had occurred in the media. Race and gender each were powerful symbols, present on the show as they had been in the media during the hearings. Yet the intersection of the two, made relevant by the very existence of Hill—an African American woman—was rendered invisible both in the hearings and by the media coverage. In this episode, art mirrored life (which had been performed on televised hearings anyway).

The white female characters argued at length about Thomas and Hill, using as their frame of reference the issue of sexual harassment. The white women did (or did not) identify with Hill as a *woman*, but failed to ever mention the possible impact of her race on her experience. She became again a woman unmodified, unable to avail herself of the unspoken referent "white." She was without a race in art as she had been during the hearings.

Paralleling this distillation of Anita Hill into a raceless woman was the Black male character's commentary on Clarence Thomas. He suggested that Thomas was not qualified, citing the poor American Bar Association report card Thomas had received.[22] He did not mention the harassment issue or his view of the allegations by Hill. He saw the issue as one of race, commenting that although Bush had denied it, Thomas's race was all that the administration evidently liked about him.

Interrupting the dialogue in the middle of the show, the confirmation vote was taken, and Thomas was confirmed. Two of the white female characters responded that "women everywhere" were mad. They apparently did not perceive that this issue, being about both race *and* gender, would potentially arouse the rage of *Black* men (including their colleague) as much as it would *women*. The absence of any women of color on the show made it seem as if the angry women were all white, mirroring the media's emphasis on (white) women's reactions.

But the absence of the perspective of a Black woman on *Designing Women* merely reflected the almost complete absence of the Black female voice from the political discourse. In the law of discrimination, Black women have been forced to choose between claims of racial and sexual discrimination. Courts doctrinally have resisted the reality that discrimination or harassment can occur *because* one is a woman of color. Once the choice between race and gender can be forced, then sex can be represented by white women and race by Black men. Although Anita Hill's face is shown, her voice is not heard during the show. Thus art mirrored life again as Hill's voice was distilled and filtered such that her views could be represented by white women and a Black man, but not by herself.

Other reflections from popular politics appeared in the show as well. The Black male character was silent through much of the show; during the female characters' dialogue, there were frequent shots of his unspeaking face. When he did talk it was to speak first briefly about his lack of respect for Thomas. When he spoke later, on the subject of sexual harassment, his comments were dismissed. He described how, like Hill, he felt victimized by the repeated sexual references and comments of his female bosses. They were reluctant to believe him, and the older white female character made references to his anatomy: "Is it true what they say about Black men?" He "joked" back that it was true, serving to reinforce this horrible stereotype and to suggest to the viewer that it did not cause him pain.

He also appeared to undermine his own claim of harassment. He subsequently tried to get a white man to support his assessment, presumably for credibility, but was shown to have bribed him, which undermined the seriousness of his harassment charge (and by implication Hill's?). His concern about sexual harassment was dismissed via laugh track. His perceived need for corroboration by the second (white) man, the harassment by one character, and the aura of skepticism surrounding his claim positioned the entire discussion within a context of racial stereotypes about Black men and sexist stereotypes about sexual harassment. As in the hearings, the presence and power of these stereotypes were left unchallenged and unaddressed.

In a troubling conclusion, the feminist characters appeared in a stage version of *Whatever Happened to Baby Jane?* Oddly, the characters on the show were styled as Bette Davis and Joan Crawford rather than simply as the characters from the script, and remained in costume as Crawford and Davis for the rest of the show. They were angry about the confirmation, and the aura of Crawford and Davis made them "feel macho." This bizarre construction of Crawford and Davis as signifiers of bitchy boldness, an image of them painted in the 1940s, was unexpected in a show attempting a fair portrayal of women's issues in the 1990s.

Finally, at the pajama party, the character dressed as a crazed Davis, face stage-painted white, thrust herself in front of a television news camera to rant over the Thomas confirmation. This ending was an injustice to the feminism of the *Designing Women* character as well as a disservice to Davis. Feminists, Davis, and Crawford were portrayed through a 1940s Hollywood masculinist lens. When they decided to dance together, the fact that they both wanted to lead was passed off as a joke. The episode's final scene used symbols to convey that nothing had changed in the status quo. The sole Black man was forced to continue dancing with one of the women, serving as a small reminder of the issue that will not go away. Yet race as a symbol had been presented as almost invisible again. The feminists, costumed as bitches, danced with each other. The world of *Designing Women* went on without any resolution of the credibility dispute, other than the imprimatur of the Senate, confirming Thomas. And finally, the show ended with the words of the President at the swearing-in ceremony that "All men are created equal." These words resonated over the image of a silent (and silenced) Anita Hill. Yet all the characters were at a party together. As a community that coexists, we, like these characters, must continue to work to understand and change the dynamics of racism and sexism, and their intersection.

The Legacy of Doubt

After watching the televised Senate hearings, each member of society should be extremely frightened about the Senate's insensitivity to the needs and lives of the majority of its constituency, women. This concern should also prompt examination of the Senate's record on broader gender and racial issues. Can the powerless in this country truly have a represented voice when all the authority to which the Senate defers is male, white, heterosexual, and economically privileged?

After the allegations brought by Anita Hill became public, many watched in disbelief, realizing that our representative institution was in fact filled with people who did not or would not comprehend the substance and standards of sex discrimination law. As they proved in their comments to the press and in their questioning of Hill, few, if any, members of the Senate Judiciary Committee know what constitutes sexual harassment. Senator Simpson distinguished sexual harassment from "real harassment." Senator Arlen Specter was unsure whether speech without physical contact was included in its ambit. The most elite electoral institution found itself floundering hopelessly when attempting to face the issue of sexism, a problem that plagues more than half of the country's citizens. Consequently, because the senators could not fathom the issue of sexism from their ocean of privilege, they certainly could not understand the intersection of sexism with racism.

More than 50 percent of the people in this country are females of all races. This fact is cited every time feminists (men and women) suggest that political representation is uneven, insensitive, and arguably nonexistent for this special interest, which happens to be a majority. In a nation where institutions overwhelmingly cater to the interests of power and money (if these things are separable), both of which are controlled by males, it is not surprising that more women's voices are not heard. Patriarchal structures govern access to advertising, the media, banks, and most jobs. Even when women are present, such as Senator Nancy Kassebaum, it is often because they have met and adopted male standards. Thus, Senator Kassebaum was able logically to say that she resented being forced to choose between being a senator and a woman: "[T]hroughout my years here I have taken pride in the fact that I am a U.S. Senator, not a woman Senator."[23] She unwittingly pointed out that a hidden referent in "senator" is male.

Media and money are all-important to politicians as they seek "image" and financing in their quest for constituents and power bases. Neither the media nor the economic institutions of the country have tended to value women for much other than as commodities used to sell most everything from beer to cars. Struggles for true valuation in areas such as comparable worth and child care and in corporate positions have proved elusive.

Thus, to say that the Senate is male means not only that nearly all of its members are men, but also that its values and abstractions derive from male perspectives that influence its definitions of power and empowerment, and ultimately freedom. This should make women and feminist men across the country nervous as civil rights advocates reluctantly turn away from the federal courts and toward the legislatures for protection of the wavering right to reproductive freedom, the formulation of a national child care policy, and a forum to address issues of battery and rape within and without the home as well as sexual harassment. Why are these policies and laws, which are crucial to women's lives, given such short shrift in legislative forums?

Clarence Thomas joins a Supreme Court that is often described as conservative. Yet it has acted as a very radical body, overturning precedent without compunction.[24] Thomas's confirmation has not eased doubts about him, about the Senate, or ultimately about the system of justice. Is there a person in this nation who believes that Clarence Thomas never discussed *Roe v. Wade* with anyone?[25] Is there a person in this nation who believed Bush when he said that Thomas was the best-qualified person for the job and that race had nothing to do with his nomination?[26] As Thomas played the race card, a card he had proclaimed was not in his deck, he raised more questions: How could he have been treated better? Should the claims of African American women be ignored when they are brought against African American men (as they frequently are)? Most important, how can society prevent the misuse of race? As we sift among the symbols, how many more doubts do we have?

Chapter 5

Trina Grillo and
Stephanie M. Wildman

Obscuring the Importance of Race

The Implication of Making
Comparisons between Racism
and Sexism (or Other Isms)

Prologue

Between the time this chapter was first solicited and its initial publication, one of the authors, Trina Grillo, who is of Afro-Cuban and
Italian descent, was diagnosed as having Hodgkin's disease (a form of
cancer) and has undergone radiation therapy. In talking about this
experience she said that "cancer has become the first filter through

An earlier version of this chapter appeared as Trina Grillo and Stephanie M. Wildman,
*Obscuring the Importance of Race: The Implication of Making Comparisons between
Racism and Sexism (or Other -Isms)*, 1991 DUKE L. J. 397, copyright © 1991 by Trina
Grillo and Stephanie M. Wildman. Reprinted with permission. The Duke editors
changed the word "heterosexism" to "homosexualism" without the consent of the
authors in that publication. The text appears here in its correct form.
   The article also refers to Trina Grillo's first bout with cancer. Since the article was pub-
lished she has continued to struggle with the illness.

which I see the world. It used to be race, but now it is cancer. My neighbor just became pregnant, and all I could think was 'How could she get pregnant? What if she gets cancer?'"

Stephanie Wildman, the coauthor, who is Jewish and white, heard this remark and thought, "I understand how she feels; I worry about getting cancer too. I probably worry about it more than most people, because I am such a worrier."

But Stephanie's worry is not the same as Trina's. Someone with cancer can think of nothing else. She cannot watch the World Series without wondering which players have had cancer or who in the players' families might have cancer. Having this worldview with cancer as a filter is different from just thinking or even worrying often about cancer. The worrier has the privilege of forgetting the worry sometimes, even much of the time. The worry can be turned off. The cancer patient does not have the privilege of truly forgetting about her cancer; even when it is not in the forefront of her thoughts, it remains in the background, coloring her world.

This dialogue about cancer illustrates a principal problem with comparing one's situation to another's. The "analogizer" often believes that her situation is the same as another's. Nothing in the comparison process challenges this belief, and the analogizer may think she understands the other's situation in its fullness. The analogy makes the analogizer forget the difference and allows her to stay focused on her own situation without grappling with the other person's reality.

Yet analogies are necessary tools to teach and explain, so that we can better understand each others' experiences and realities. We have no other way to understand each others' lives, except by making analogies to events in our own experience. Thus, the use of analogies provides both the key to greater comprehension and the danger of false understanding.

Racism/White Supremacy as Social Ill

Like cancer, racism/white supremacy is a societal illness. To people of color, who are the victims of racism/white supremacy, race is a filter through which they see the world. Whites do not look at the world through this filter of racial awareness, even though they also constitute a race. This privilege to ignore their race gives whites a societal advantage distinct from any advantage received from the existence of discriminatory racism. Throughout this chapter we use the term "racism/white supremacy" to emphasize the link between discriminatory racism and the privilege held by whites to ignore their own race.

The author bell hooks describes her realization of the connection between these two concepts: "The word racism ceased to be the term which best expressed for me exploitation of black people and other people of color in this society and . . . I began to understand that the most useful term was white supremacy."[1] As noted in Chapter 1, hooks has observed that liberal whites do not see themselves as prejudiced or interested in domination through coercion, and do not acknowledge the ways they contribute to and benefit from the system of white privilege.[2] For these reasons, "white supremacy" is an important term, descriptive of American social reality. In this chapter, we link the term "racism" to "white supremacy" as a reminder that the perpetuation of white supremacy is racist. (Although the perpetuation of white supremacy is racist, we do not believe that most whites *want* to be racist or white supremacist.)

This chapter originated when the authors noticed that several identifiable phenomena occurred without fail, in any predominantly white racially mixed group, whenever sex discrimination was analogized (implicitly or explicitly) to race discrimination. Repeatedly, at the annual meeting of the Association of American Law Schools (AALS), at meetings of feminist legal scholars, in classes on sex discrimination and the law, and in law school women's caucus meetings, the pattern was the same. In each setting, although the analogy was made for the purpose of illumination, to explain sexism and sex discrimination, another unintended result ensued—the perpetuation of racism/white supremacy.

When a speaker compared sexism and racism, the significance of race was marginalized and obscured, and the different role that race plays in the lives of people of color and whites was overlooked. The concerns of whites became the focus of discussion, even when the conversation had supposedly centered on race discrimination. Essentialist presumptions became implicit in the discussion: it would be assumed, for example, that "women" referred to white women and "Blacks" meant African American men.[3] Finally, people with little experience in thinking about racism/white supremacy, but who had a hard-won understanding of the allegedly analogous oppression (sexism or some other ism), assumed that they comprehended the experience of people of color and thus had standing to speak on their behalf.

No matter how carefully a setting was structured to address the question of racism/white supremacy, these problems always arose. Each of the authors has unwittingly participated in creating these problems on many occasions, yet when we have tried to avoid them, we have found ourselves accused of making others uncomfortable. Even after we had identified these patterns, we found ourselves watching in amazement as they appeared again and again, and we were unable to keep ourselves from contributing to them.

We began to question why this pattern persisted. We concluded that these phenomena have much to do with the dangers inherent in what had previously seemed to us to be a creative and solidarity-producing process—analogizing sex discrimination to race discrimination. These dangers were obscured by the promise that to discuss and compare oppressions might lead to coalition building and understanding. On an individual psychological level, we empathize with and understand others by comparing their situations with some aspects of our own. As Lynne Henderson explains,

> Analogizing, or drawing upon one's own experience to under-
> stand another's feelings or experiences, is a part of relating to

another, if for no other reason than that no one has exactly the same experiences as anyone else. But this is an obvious point. The less obvious point is that it is possible to draw on one's own similar experiences to understand another. One could otherwise not empathize with another's grief at losing a parent at all if one could not draw on one's own experiences of loss.[4]

Roberto Unger describes the importance of analogy in the human thought process as follows:

> We compare the issues about which we have the greatest certainty with those that baffle us more. The decision to liken one instance to another, or to distinguish them, turns on a judgment of what differences and similarities are most significant to the moral beliefs at stake.[5]

Thus, analogies deepen our consciousness and permit us to progress in our thinking. Analogies are an important, perhaps indispensable, tool in individual moral reasoning.

This chapter represents our effort to understand how the process of comparing oppressions creates the phenomena that consolidate racism/white supremacy. We believe that the participants in the meetings we have described, who used analogies between sexism and racism, were well intentioned. They were people with antiracist politics and no desire to perpetuate racism/white supremacy. But even well-intentioned people may act unwittingly to maintain racism/white supremacy.[6]

Although the central focus of this chapter is the analogy between sexism and racism, we also discuss comparisons with other "isms," including anti-Semitism, heterosexism, and the treatment of the physically challenged. The use of these comparisons further illuminates the analogy problem because the issues surrounding the use of analogies exist for these isms as well.

How the Sex/Race Analogy Perpetuates Patterns of
   Racial Domination

Comparing sexism to racism perpetuates patterns of racial domination by minimizing the impact of racism, rendering it an insignificant phenomenon—one of a laundry list of isms or oppressions that society must suffer. This marginalization and obfuscation is evident in three recognizable patterns: (1) the taking back of center stage from people of color, even in discussions of racism, so that white issues remain or become central in the dialogue; (2) the fostering of essentialism, so that women and people of color are implicitly viewed as belonging to mutually exclusive categories, rendering women of color invisible; and (3) the appropriation of pain or the denial of its existence that results when whites who have compared other oppressions to race discrimination believe they understand the experience of racism.

A. *Taking Back the Center*

White supremacy creates in whites the expectation that issues of concern to them will be central in every discourse. Analogies serve to perpetuate this expectation of centrality. The center stage problem occurs because dominant group members are already accustomed to being center stage. They have been treated that way by society; it feels natural, comfortable, and in the order of things.

The harms of discrimination include not only the easily identified disadvantages of the victims (such as exclusion from housing and jobs) and the stigma imposed by the dominant culture, but also the advantages given to those who are not its victims. The white, male, heterosexual societal norm is privileged in such a way that its privilege is rendered invisible. As Kimberlè Crenshaw explained,

> According to a dominant view, a discriminator treats all people
> within a race or sex category similarly. Any significant experi-

ential or statistical variation within this group suggests . . . that the group is not being discriminated against. . . . Race and sex, moreover, become significant only when they operate to explicitly *disadvantage* the victims; because the *privileging* of whiteness or maleness is implicit, it is generally not perceived at all.[7]

Because whiteness is the norm, it is easy to forget that it is not the only perspective. Thus, members of dominant groups assume that their perceptions are the pertinent perceptions, that their problems are the problems that need to be addressed, and that in discourse they should be the speaker rather than the listener. Part of being a member of a privileged group is being the center and the subject of all inquiry in which people of color or other nonprivileged groups are the objects.

So strong is this expectation of holding center stage that even when a time and place are specifically designated for members of a nonprivileged group to be central, members of the dominant group will often attempt to take back the pivotal focus. They are stealing the center—usually with a complete lack of self-consciousness.[8]

This phenomenon occurred at the annual meeting of Law and Society, where three scholars, all people of color, were invited to speak to the plenary session about how universities might become truly multicultural. Even before the dialogue began, the views of many members of the organization were apparent by their presence or absence at the session. The audience included nearly every person of color who was attending the meeting, yet many whites chose not to attend.

When people who are not regarded as entitled to the center move into it, however briefly, they are viewed as usurpers. One reaction of the group temporarily deprived of the center is to make sure that nothing remains for the perceived usurpers to be in the center of. Thus, the whites who did not attend the plenary session, but who would have attended had there been more traditional (i.e., white) speakers, did so in part because they were exercising their privilege not to think in terms of race, and in part because they resented the "out groups" having the center.

Another tactic used by the dominant group is to steal back the center, using guerrilla tactics where necessary. For example, during a talk devoted to the integration of multicultural materials into the core curriculum, a white man got up from the front row and walked noisily to the rear of the room. He then paced the room in a distracting fashion and finally returned to his seat. During the question period he was the first to rise, leaping to his feet to ask a lengthy, rambling question about how multicultural materials could be added to university curricula without disturbing the "canon"—the exact subject of the talk he had just, apparently, not listened to.

The speaker answered politely and explained how he had assigned a Navajo creation myth to accompany St. Augustine, which highlighted some similarities between Augustine's thought and pre-Christian belief systems and resulted in each reading enriching the other. He refrained, however, from calling attention to the questioner's rude behavior during the meeting, to his asking the already-answered question, or to his presumption that the material the questioner saw as most relevant to his own life was central and "canonized," while all other reading was peripheral and, hence, dispensable.

Analogies offer protection for the traditional center. At another gathering of law professors—the annual meeting of the American Association of Law Schools—issues of racism, sexism, and homophobia were the focus of the plenary session for the first time in the organization's history. Again at this session, far fewer white males were present than would ordinarily attend the organization's plenary session. After moving presentations by an African American woman, a Latino man, and a gay white man, who each opened their hearts on these subjects, a question and dialogue period began.

The first speaker to rise was a white woman, who, after saying that she did not mean to change the topic, said that she wanted to discuss another sort of oppression—that of law professors in the less elite schools. As professors from what is perceived by some as a less-than-elite school, we agree that the topic is important and it would have interested us at another time, on another day. But this questioner had succeeded in depriving the other issues of time devoted (after much struggle) specifically to them, and turned the spotlight once again onto her own concerns. She did this, we believe, not out of malice, but because she too had become a victim of analogical thinking.

The problem of taking back the center exists apart from the issue of analogies; it will be with us as long as any group expects, and is led to expect, to be constantly the center of attention. But the use of analogies exacerbates this problem, for once an analogy is taken to heart, it seems to the center-stealer that she is *not* stealing the center, but rather is continuing the discussion on the same topic, and one that she knows well. So when the format of the program implicitly analogized gender and sexual preference to race, the center-stealer was encouraged to think, "Why not go further to another perceived oppression?"

When socially subordinated groups are lumped together, oppression begins to look like a uniform problem, and one may neglect the varying and complex contexts of the different groups being addressed. If oppression is all the same, then we are all equally able to discuss each oppression, and there is no felt need for us to listen to and learn from other socially subordinated groups.

B. Fostering Essentialism

Essentialism is implicit in analogies between sex and race. Angela Harris explains gender essentialism as "[t]he notion that there is a monolithic 'women's experience' that can be described independent of other facets of experience like race, class, and sexual orientation."[9]

She continues: "A corollary to gender essentialism is 'racial essentialism'—the belief that there is a monolithic 'Black Experience,' or 'Chicano Experience.'"[10]

To analogize gender to race, one must assume that each is a distinct category, the impact of which can be neatly separated, one from the other. The essentialist critique shows that this division is not possible. Whenever it is attempted, the experience of women of color, who are at the intersection of these categories and cannot divide themselves to compare their own experiences, is rendered invisible. Analogizing sex discrimination to race discrimination makes it seem that all the women are white and all the men are African American.[11] "Moreover, feminist essentialism represents not just an insult to black women, but a broken promise—the promise to listen to women's stories, the promise of feminist method."[12]

C. The Appropriation of Pain or the Rejection of Its Existence

Many whites think that people of color are obsessed with race and find it hard to understand the emotional and intellectual energy that people of color devote to the subject. But white supremacy privileges whiteness as the normative model. Being the norm allows whites to ignore race, even though they have one, except when they perceive race (usually someone else's) as intruding upon their lives.[13]

Whites need to reject this privilege and recognize and speak about their role in the racial hierarchy. Yet whites cannot speak validly for people of color, but only about their own experiences as whites. Comparing other oppressions to race gives whites a false sense that they fully understand the experience of people of color. Sometimes the profession of understanding by members of a privileged group may even be a guise for a rejection of the existence of the pain of the unprivileged. For people of color, listening to whites who purport to represent the experience of racism feels like an appropriation of the pain of living in a world of racism/white supremacy.

The privileging of some groups in society over others is a fact of contemporary American life. This privileging is identifiable in the ordering of societal power between whites and people of color; men and women; heterosexuals and gays and lesbians; and able-bodied and physically challenged people. This societal ordering is clear to children as early as kindergarten.[14]

Judy Scales-Trent has written about her own experience as an African American woman, of "being black and looking white," a woman who thereby inhabits both sides of the privilege dichotomy.[15] As one who was used to being on the unprivileged side of the race dichotomy in some aspects of her life, she discusses how the privilege of being able-bodied allowed her to ignore the pain of an unprivileged woman in a wheelchair, humiliated in seeking access to a meeting place.[16] She realized that her role as the privileged one in that pairing likened her to whites in the racial pairing. The analogy helped her see the role of privilege and how it affects us, presenting another example of how comparisons are useful for promoting understanding. But this insight did not lead her to assume that she could speak for those who are physically challenged; rather, she realized that she needed to listen more carefully.

Not all people who learn about others' oppressions through analogy are blessed with an increased commitment to listening. White people who grasp an analogy between an oppression they have suffered and race discrimination may think they understand the phenomenon of racism/white supremacy in all its aspects. They may believe that their opinions and judgments about race are as cogent as those of victims of racism. In this circumstance, something approximating a lack of standing to speak exists, because the insight gained by personal experience cannot easily be duplicated—certainly not without careful study of the oppression under scrutiny.[17] The power of comparisons undermines this lack of standing, because by emphasizing similarity and obscuring difference, it permits the speaker implicitly to demonstrate authority about both forms of oppression. If we are members of the privileged halves of the social pairs, then what we say about the dichotomy will be listened to by the dominant culture. Thus, when we employ analogies to teach and to show oppression in a particular situation, we should be careful that in borrowing the acknowledged and clear oppression, we do not neutralize it, or make it appear fungible with the oppression under discussion.

The use of analogies by whites allows them to focus on their own experience and avoid working on understanding racism/white supremacy. Even whites who wish to end discrimination want people of color to teach them about race and are often unwilling to use their personal resources to explore this dangerous subject. As bell hooks has written,

> In talking about race and gender recently, the question most often asked by white women has to do with white women's response to black women or women of color insisting that they are not willing to teach them about their racism—to show the way. They want to know: What should a white person do who is attempting to resist racism? It is problematic to assert that black people and other people of color who are sincerely committed to struggling against white supremacy should be unwilling to help or teach white people.[18]

She says that many people of color have responded with an unwillingness to teach whites about combating racism/white supremacy because it often seems that white people are asking people of color to do all the work. She concludes, however, that "[i]t is our collective responsibility as people of color and as white people who are committed to ending white supremacy to help one another."[19]

hooks encourages people of color to continue to struggle with whites about racism. To whites, the need for such encouragement may seem surprising, because many whites might ask, "How can we work on racism by ourselves, without people of color?" Listening to the reality of people of color *is* very important for learning about the oppression of racism/white supremacy. But whites need to examine their (our) own role in benefiting from that social construct. When white women analogize sexism to racism to emphasize the disadvantages society imposes on women, they (we) must also remember the privileging granted to whites by that same society.

Trying to educate whites about race is a great risk for people of color. They risk not only that whites will not care and will prefer to perpetuate the status quo, but also that even caring whites will not hear or understand the pain of racism. Talking about racism/white supremacy is painful for whites as well, but in a different way. Whites must confront their role as oppressors, or at least as beneficiaries of the racial oppression of others, in a race-based hierarchy. The pain of oppression must be communicated to the dominant group if there is to be any understanding of racism/white supremacy. This act of sharing, however, contains the risk that the pain of oppression will be appropriated by the dominant group for its own purpose.

This appropriation of pain occurred during a critical legal studies summer camp devoted to a discussion of gender and race. A Native Canadian woman realized that her life experience as a dispossessed person bearing the sting of racism/white supremacy had been dissected by the group and that no one was really hearing or responding to her pain, and stated,

> I had gone away for this conference quite settled with having to deal with racism, pure and simple. But, I was not ready to have my pain appropriated. I am pretty possessive about my pain. It is my pain. I worked hard for it. Some days it is all I have. Some days it is the only thing I can feel. Do not try to take that away from me too.[20]

This woman protested the appropriation of her pain by others who would objectify and minimize it.[21]

Many people at the summer camp seemed concerned that their own pain might be overlooked.[22] We share a primal, and not unreasonable, fear that if we open ourselves enough to comprehend another's pain, we will lose our right to feel our own, especially if ours cannot compete in the pain sweepstakes. How can one compare the problems of, for example, an untenured white male professor with those of undernourished Native American children, whose people have been the victims of genocide?[23] And yet, as long as we are human, the first filter through which we look will be the one constructed by the events of our individual lives.

The use of analogy exacerbates this natural desire to have our own struggles receive recognition. For if we can convince ourselves that another's experience is "just like" ours, we are then exempt from having fully to comprehend that experience.

When I (Trina) was in law school, the women in the women's caucus, all white except for me, insisted that sexism was "worse than" racism. I disagreed (as one who should know) and pointed out that women of color generally find racism harder to deal with than sexism. The famous statement to the contrary by Shirley Chisholm was raised, and the argument ended.[24]

The interesting part of this interchange was that if these women could show that sexism was worse than racism, then ("hallelujah!") they believed their reason to worry about racism had vanished. The women thought that they understood racism by virtue of their experiences with sexism and that they were working on something more important.

The use of the sex/race analogy gave the analogizers permission to make invisible and unimportant experiences that were central to the lives of others. This resulted in a denial of the existence of pain. Thus, both the appropriation of pain and the denial of its existence are fostered by comparing oppressions. Moreover, this attitude creates problems for those of us who have both battles to fight—battles that are not separable in our personal lives.

Toward Using Analogies Ethically: Recognition Time and Coalition Work

Given the problems that analogies create and perpetuate, should we ever use them? Analogies can be helpful. They are part of legal discourse, as well as common conversation. Consciousness-raising may be the beginning of knowledge. Starting with ourselves is important, and analogies may enable us to understand the oppression of another in a way we could not without making the comparison. It is important for whites to talk about white supremacy—rather than leaving all the work for people of color—and without drawing false inferences of similarities from analogies. Questions remain regarding whether we can make analogies to race, particularly in legal argument, without reinforcing racism/white supremacy. There are no simple answers to this thorny problem. We will have to continue to struggle with it, and accept that our progress will be slow and tentative. We offer two preliminary suggestions, each with its own pitfalls, to illustrate the sort of changes we might make in daily discourse to guide the use of comparisons: recognition time and coalition work.

Recognition time is time devoted exclusively to examining one oppression. It may mitigate one problem created when we make analogies to race—the marginalizing and obscuring of racism/white supremacy. Recognition time acknowledges both the need to honor the pain of those oppressed by other isms, each in their turn, and the need to allow the oppression being focused on to remain center stage.

Creating recognition time may not be easy, and it raises problems of its own. An African American woman law professor who teaches a seminar on women of color and the law has said that she finds it difficult to focus the students on gender issues; they want to stay with race. Why might this happen? If the first filter through which one looks at the world is not acknowledged, one cannot move on to other, perhaps even equally important, filters. When we combine several socially subordinated groups into one discussion (as analogies implicitly do) and do not set aside a distinct time to recognize one specific oppression or another, other than to use them as reference points for an analogy, we create an inability to focus on any one of them. This does not mean that the oppressions are unrelated, but rather, that they must be studied separately as well as together. To allow these separate and focused recognition times might relax people.

The danger of recognition time, if defined too narrowly, is that it would encourage essentialism. Essentialism could be avoided if each oppression were examined in its fullness. In discussing sexism, for example, we need to recognize that every woman is affected by racism/white supremacy in one way or another. Within the context of a full discussion of sexual oppression, one would necessarily talk about the effect of race.

For people facing oppression, working together or coalition building is also critically important. In a racism course at one law school, I (Stephanie) was asked to team-teach a session on Jewish racism and African American anti-Semitism. The Jewish students felt that anti-Semitic remarks had been made throughout the semester and that neither the law school's curriculum nor its culture addressed issues of anti-Semitism. The students of color felt that during the one course in the curriculum designed to address their issues, the white students once again had taken the airwaves from the students of color for their own purpose. Both groups were correct. Coalition work is essential to make sure that each group gets access to the airwaves.[25]

A fundamental tension exists whenever analogies are used to compare other oppressions to racism. The comparison perpetuates racism/white supremacy, but is also a necessary tool to teach about the oppression being compared. Any analogy to race must be used ethically and with care. We must always consider whether we are perpetuating or deconstructing societal racism at the conclusion of any analogy discussion.

Epilogue

Today, the Sunday before Yom Kippur, I (Stephanie) go with my parents to my children's Sunday school for the closing service. The rabbi is explaining to the children the meaning of Yom Kippur, the holiest Jewish day, the Day of Atonement. "It is the day," he explains, "when we think of how we could have been better and reconsider what we did that wasn't wonderful."

He tells a story of two men who came to the rabbi before Yom Kippur. The first man said he felt very guilty and unclean and could never be cleansed, because he had once raised a stick and hurt someone. The second man said he could not think of anything very terrible he had done and that he felt pretty good. The rabbi told the first man to go to the field and bring back the largest rock he could find. He told the second man to fill his pockets with pebbles and bring them back to the synagogue, too.

The first man found a boulder and with much difficulty carried it to the rabbi. The second man filled his pockets with pebbles, brought them to the rabbi, and emptied his pockets. Pebbles scattered everywhere.

Then the rabbi said to the first man, "Now you must carry the rock back and put it back where you found it." To the second man he said, "And you too must gather up all the pebbles and return them to where you found them."

"But how can I do that? That is impossible," said the second man.

The rabbi telling the story says that the pebbles are like all the things you have done for which you should wish forgiveness—you have not noticed them, nor kept track.

And so the rabbi reminds the children that they should consider when they had ever done things that they should not have done.

He then asks them what looks different in the synagogue. The covering of the dais had been changed to white, which he explains is for purity and cleanliness. He asks the children to stand to see the special Torah covers, also white to symbolize atonement and cleanliness.

My mother leans over to me at this point and says, "Can you imagine how someone Black feels, hearing a story like this?"

Although no one in the temple was intending to be racist/white supremacist, the conversation could have had that effect, privileging whiteness in a society that is already racist/white supremacist. Is that racism the large rock, the boulder? It must seem truly that large and intractable to people of color. It seems like a boulder to me, when I think consciously about it. Yet it seems that as whites we treat our own racism like so many little pebbles; part of our privilege is that it may seem unimportant to us. So many times we are racist, privileging whiteness, and do not even realize it, and so cannot acknowledge it or atone for it, or even attempt to change our behavior. We, like the second man, say we are not racist, because it is our wish not to be. But wishing cannot make it so. The sooner we can see the boulder *and* the pebbles, the sooner we can try to remove them.

Chapter 6

Stephanie M. Wildman

The Dream of Diversity and the Cycle of Exclusion

The racial transformation of society envisioned in Martin Luther King's dream has been an emotional and powerful ideal. That vision has gone through its own transformation: it was first described as "integration," then "affirmative action," and then "diversity" and "multiculturalism." As each of these phrases acquired negative connotation from reactionary, conservative backlashes, a new phrase has had to be invented to carry forward that transformative vision. Yet the cycle of exclusion that privileges the dominant cultural status quo continues.

An earlier version of this chapter appeared as Stephanie M. Wildman, *Integration in the 1980s: The Dream of Diversity and the Cycle of Exclusion*, 64 TULANE LAW REVIEW 1625 (1990), copyright © 1990 by the Tulane Law Review Association. Reprinted with permission.

One place, close to home, where the dream of integration has not been fulfilled is the cloister of legal academia. This chapter singles out legal education to illustrate the dream of integration and the cycle of exclusion, examining the small group dynamics that serve to maintain the dominant status quo. A description of the issues, as they arise in legal academia, provides an example that many lawyers, judges, and professors know well and portrays the complexity of the exclusionary dynamic.

The legal academy serves as the gateway to the legal profession. The academy and the profession remain primarily white and male; the gatekeepers to this still segregated domain are the legal academicians. The harm of segregation has been clearly recognized by modern judges. Judge John Minor Wisdom, the author of many leading desegregation decisions in the 1960s, described that harm as "[d]enial of access to the dominant culture, lack of opportunity in any meaningful way to participate in political and other public activities, [and] the stigma of apartheid condemned in the Thirteenth Amendment."[1] Another serious harm of segregation is that the dominant culture has no access to the insights of the segregated culture and does not even perceive this omission as a loss. The problems of denial of access, lack of opportunity, stigma, and lost insights have continued to surface as the struggle to achieve integration has continued on new battlefronts with a different vocabulary.

Judge Wisdom recognized the importance of faculty integration in the desegregation of Southern schools. No less compelling is the necessity for faculty integration at the law school level if the legal profession is to be integrated.

Nondiscrimination is the law and a goal upon which all agree in theory. This chapter examines some of the obstacles to the attainment of that goal of nondiscrimination, using the example of law school faculty hiring. Antidiscrimination law requires "victims" who file charges against "perpetrators."[2] Yet the collegial etiquette of the academy (and of many other societal institutions) requires that accusations of discrimination not be made. Even if they are made, the deliberations leading to appointments and tenure decisions are cloaked in secrecy to protect academic freedom and collegial communications.

The discrimination plaintiff, however, must pierce the protective veil or lose her case: she must articulate who said what, when, and for what purpose. Even with access to otherwise confidential files, the discrimination plaintiff may not be able to document the group dynamics that resulted in the tenuring or hiring decision. Group dynamics, which are rarely captured in written form, are hard to convey in the concrete details required for litigation. Yet these group interrelations operate as a subtext to any faculty hiring or tenure decision and can be characterized as a microlegal system.

Integrating the academy by lawsuits may be not only difficult, but also not as effective as less litigious approaches through voluntary action. Association of American Law Schools (AALS) president Herma Hill Kay reminded law school professors that three past AALS presidents have "stressed the importance and value to legal education of the commitment to achieving diversity among the faculty."[3] Kay's article described legal academia's faltering progress in recruiting and retaining professors who are people of color, women, gay, or lesbian.

Noting that members of these groups have suffered from a long history of exclusion and are entering a profession that has been "traditionally dominated by white men," Kay concluded that "those who have been the insiders must be sensitive to their unspoken assumptions about the newcomers. A commitment to diversity cannot succeed without the willingness to hear, understand, and accept their different voices."[4] Acknowledging that acceptance will not be easy, Kay reminded faculty that diversity will bring "intellectual richness" to legal education.

Kay's point that faculty diversity enhances the educational institution is important. Many view the goal of affirmative action, or diversity (as it is now often called in order to avoid the stigma associated with the term "affirmative action"), as one of aesthetic balance—we all need a person of color, a woman, or a gay or lesbian colleague, lest we look bad. But much more is at stake here than appearances or even our view of ourselves as nonracist, nonsexist, and nonhomophobic.

The reality of American democracy and the institutions within it is that social privileges are accorded based on race, sex, class, and sexual preference. Given the history of exclusion of women, people of color, gays, and lesbians to which Kay refers, some kind of institutional acting that is affirmative is required to overcome the effects of that exclusion. Proponents of equality must reclaim and relegitimate the notion of acting affirmatively to ensure our integration with all members of society and to end the perpetuation of the predominantly white, male, and heterosexual status quo.

This chapter seeks to tell stories about recruiting and retaining faculty members from nonmajority groups as they might really occur. While the incidents described are fictitious, any resemblance to real interaction on law school faculties is quite intentional.

Unwritten Rules

Walter O. Weyrauch has described law as a network of small group interactions in which basic characteristics of legal systems govern the interactions of individuals within small groups.[5] Paralleling law as a linking in large social group interaction, each small group has its own operating principles and generates, through its own group dynamics, proper rules of behavior for members in the group. Weyrauch studied the interaction of nine men, who participated in a three-month nutrition experiment, isolated in a Berkeley penthouse. He observed normative behavior that he described as the basic law or constitutional document of the group. This behavioral constitution expressed "some form of understanding based on shared ideals."[6]

The foremost canon of a group's dynamic is that the "rules are not to be articulated." This rule, that the group not identify and articulate its own rules, occurs on law faculties as well as in experimental groups. Although Weyrauch's work has been criticized for focusing on the group's own rule system, "rather than on ascertaining internal effects of external rules,"[7] his study showed that the external social realities of racism and sexism affected the rules of the group. Weyrauch found ethnic prejudices within the context of group dynamics, even among a group professing to be "highly liberal about civil rights."

Describing some of the laws of this penthouse group, Weyrauch observed, "Equality of all persons is espoused, but women are not really treated as equal (rules 5 and 7); racial and religious discriminations are outlawed, but if they occur the fact of their existence is to be denied (rule 9)." The rules to which the above passage refers are rules of the particular group Weyrauch studied, not necessarily rules of all small groups. Nonetheless, in his group's unspoken rules that both espouse equality and deny the existence of discrimination, we see an example of the silence surrounding the systems of privilege that permeate our culture and the small groups within it. This silence about privilege ensures its perpetuation. Antidiscrimination law encourages this silence by not noticing the operation of privilege. Law faculties have further incentive to deny that discrimination has occurred to avoid liability in an employment discrimination suit.

To enter academia and advance in it, one must know the "rules of the game." It has been observed that "All institutions operate through a set of formal and informal rules. . . . [T]he rules for entry into the profession are fairly straightforward. . . . The rules for employment and professional advancement, however, are harder to define, varying with the kind of institution, the region, and the times."[8] The same can be said about law, since to become a lawyer and to enter the profession, one must pass a bar exam; but to become a law professor, the institution, region, and times affect the "qualifications."

The study of small group dynamics has important ramifications for hiring decisions generally and for law school hiring in particular. The dynamics of sex, race, and heterosexual privilege, which are social realities in contemporary America, interface with the rules of each faculty group as the hiring decision is made, but at a level so far beneath the surface that the decisions are insulated from review. The absence of procedural or constitutional protection for the hiring process, as well as the absence of hard and fast rules, make it particularly difficult to change the group dynamics or prove discrimination. The privileging of whiteness, maleness, and heterosexuality is the "rule" that exists outside the group and becomes incorporated into the group dynamic. Thus the legal doctrine is unable to adequately address the reality of the situation—the subtlety of discrimination and the deeply hidden levels on which it occurs.

The group dynamic of self-perpetuation predominates over any sense of urgency about the need for integration or diversification. The need to act affirmatively to change the status quo is not a felt need in the context of the group. For those in no rush, the legal doctrine's inability to reach the deep layers of group interaction is an advantage. Yet the metaphor of an ambulance, which breaks the law by traveling through traffic signals to render emergency aid, more aptly suggests the kind of response the legal system should take to privilege and discrimination in American society.

When law faculty talk about hiring, certain criteria and phrases are an accepted part of the discourse, which ostensibly is about the qualifications of the applicant. No one wants to hire an applicant who is not qualified. And so participants in the discourse tacitly agree that the conversation is about evaluating qualifications and eliminating the unqualified.

But the conversation that is really going on is not at all about qualifications. The discussants are asking, "Will this person fit into our group, fit into our institution? Will this person change it in any way that will make me not fit, or hurt my place in the institution in any way? If someone comes who is not like me, will I still be valued at this place, at other places, or have other opportunities?"

"Mirror, mirror, on the wall, who's the fairest of them all?" We are all familiar with the fairy tale chant (can beauty be dark in this tale?). The queen is pleased as long as the mirror answers her question, "You, your majesty," but she flies into a jealous rage, when the mirror says, "Snow White."[9] When the "other" is named the most valuable, the dominant power self-destructs. At some subliminal level, do the culturally dominant fear that the introduction of difference represents their destruction, from either themselves or the outside?

Derrick Bell has recognized this problem in his discussion of the tipping point issue; for the dominant group the presence of a few minorities is acceptable, but too many will tip the balance at which the dominant group feels comfortable. The hiring discourse tries to place someone on the scale to measure where that person will weigh in relation to the tipping point. Will the candidate really be one of the good old (implicitly white, male, straight) boys?

The faculty debate uses words in the discourse that involve qualifications; and one must answer in the words they have established for that discourse, rather than say, "She's okay; she won't hurt you." And so rather than speak the words that the group is truly worried about, we argue about whether she is really qualified.

Group dynamics intersect with systems of privilege to tacitly reinforce the presence and power of those systems. Since we have no permission in the group dynamic to discuss even the existence of these systems, they inevitably remain. The dominant group retains its sense of entitlement to group leadership and its deeply held belief that the leader's vision of the world is the only correct one. The inclusion and recognition of multiple perspectives would provide some antidote to the dominance of systems of privilege within the group dynamic.

A Story about Tradition

"Harold, what will it take to get your vote? I know you're a horse trader from way back." Jessica knew that her colleague appreciated a direct "cards on the table" approach to faculty politics. But what might he ask as a quid pro quo?

"There's nothing to horse trade," Harold replied. "You have no idea how upset I am at the prospect of losing Jared Daniels as a candidate for this teaching position. You know what I most care about is hiring the best possible candidate for this job." Jessica only half listened as Harold extolled the virtues of his candidate, who was, like Harold, a capable white man with a good academic record from a local law school and who had prior teaching experience. Jessica would have been happy to have him as a colleague; in fact, she would have preferred him to several of the men now on her faculty. However, there was only one job right now.

"At least," thought Jessica, "he's conceding there is a position." She reflected that many of her colleagues often emphasized how the law school must hire good people whenever a qualified white male candidate appeared on the horizon, but when the candidate was a person of color or a white woman, they questioned whether the school could really afford to hire anyone.

Jessica, a white woman, had been on the faculty appointments committee for fifteen years. She had been hired by Holmes College of Law, a well-known regional law school, in the early 1970s, along with an African American man and a Latino man. The three of them had been the affirmative action hires. The trio all had had outstanding credentials, in some cases better than those of the colleagues they were joining. That faculty had been composed only of white men. One woman of color, who had been hired some years earlier, had left.

Faced with the prospect of being an all-white, male faculty, the school had realized that it should act affirmatively and had sought female and minority colleagues.

Since joining the hiring committee, Jessica had tried to be sure that the thirty-member faculty looked at other qualified people of color and white female applicants for available teaching positions. Now, fifteen years later, there were two white women on the faculty, besides Jessica, and one African American man. The colleagues who had been hired with her had left for other institutions; one who had remained in teaching was at a Midwestern law school and one had become an appellate court judge. In that same period, five white men had been hired, in addition to the two white women and one minority man.

When Harold finished praising his candidate, Jessica said, "What about our need for affirmative action?"

"Sure," replied Harold, "I can see we need more conservative Republicans on this faculty; that view is underrepresented here."

Jessica wasn't sure what to do. She could see this would be a losing battle. Should she try to explain to Harold that underrepresentation of women and minorities on law faculties was not the same thing as not having a Republican majority on the faculty? Would Harold be able to see that the Republican viewpoint was easily accessible to students everywhere in American culture—in the news, on the radio? The mainstream culture was in no danger of being underrepresented. It was the viewpoint of those outside that culture that was in danger of being unheard.

As she left his office, Jessica promised Harold to leave him a book review by Ursula K. Le Guin and said they could talk later.

The Majoritarian Culture

Ursula K. Le Guin has written,

> We human beings long to get the world under our control and
> to make other people act just like us. In the last few centuries,

some of us—variously described as the White Man, the West, the Colonial Powers, Industrial Civilization, the March of Progress—found out how to do it. The result is that now many of us all over the world are eating hamburgers at McDonald's. Since other results include forests destroyed for pasture for the cattle to make the hamburgers, and oceans suffocated by the waste products of making plastic boxes for the hamburgers, the success of the White Man's control of the world is debatable; but his success in making other people act just like him is not. No culture that has come in contact with Western industrial culture has been unchanged by it, and most have been assimilated or annihilated, surviving only as vestigial variations in dress, cooking or ethics.[10]

This "tremendous process of acculturation"[11] has affected law school culture and legal education as well. Although it is only a microcosm of the greater social issues Le Guin describes, legal education has reflected the same instinct to make other people act just like us—the "us" being the majoritarian dominant culture. And we who are not part of that majority culture are affected by the time we spend in the institution and find ourselves playing roles that move us toward that mainstream.

The use of the term "diversity" is an acknowledgment that there might be some real value in not simply perpetuating the sameness of the forceful majoritarian culture. Yet the powerful human instinct that Le Guin describes, the need to control others and make them act "just like us," creates a felt tension within some minds between the goal of diversity and the desirability of that goal. The majoritarian pull to make others act like us is powerful, conflicting with the goal of diversity.

Law itself mirrors the conflict between the need for uniform treatment of like situations and the need to do justice when like situations may not be exactly alike. In the arena of sex discrimination jurisprudence, argument about whether men and women should be treated alike, minimizing the significance of reproductive differences between men and women, has stirred debate. Broad legal acceptance of the view that equality means minimizing differences, termed the "assimilationist view," demonstrates that even in legal arguments the urge toward uniformity is powerfully felt.

In our culture, the image of the melting pot is forceful; it speaks to the powerful positive image that assimilation carries. The message to those outside the mainstream dominant culture is "Melt in with us, be like us, or fail to do so at your peril." Diversity is the antidote to assimilation because it includes a celebration of differences and recognizes the contribution of all. People need to act affirmatively to tell a different story, one that celebrates diversity and underlines that we have not all melted together, nor do we need to.

Opening the Door

Affirmative action in the U.S. Supreme Court has had an uneven history. But the Court dynamics in the first fully considered affirmative action case, in which Allan Bakke filed a lawsuit to gain admission to the Medical School at the University of California at Davis, revealed the kind of majoritarian elite decision making that has doomed the affirmative action debate. Bakke, a white man, had applied for admission and had been denied twice; he believed the reason was that Davis Medical School set aside sixteen out of one hundred admission slots for minority candidates.

The parties to the case were limited to the white plaintiff and the challenged institution. The voices of people of color, who might have wanted to support the program, were excluded and silenced, and Bakke won at the California Supreme Court. The lone dissenter, Justice Mathew O. Tobriner, wrote, "There is, indeed, a very sad irony to the fact that the first admission program aimed at promoting diversity to be struck down under the Fourteenth Amendment is the program most consonant with the underlying purposes of the Fourteenth Amendment."[12] The purposes to which Tobriner referred were the eradication and remedying of past discrimination. Interestingly, the phrase "reverse discrimination," which was much used in the popular press to describe suits brought by white plaintiffs who felt harmed by affirmative action efforts, implicitly recognizes this first discrimination (i.e., against racial minorities) that the Supreme Court has declined to acknowledge by its ultimate refusal to accept the reality of societal discrimination as a reason for affirmative action.

Charles Lawrence has described the arguments before the U.S. Supreme Court as a "discussion among gentlemen."[13] Archibald Cox, a white Harvard professor who represented the University of California, had been chosen over several Black attorneys whom minority groups had urged as the logical choice. Lawrence explains, "The regents wanted to make it clear that their lawyer represented the university and higher education and not the interests of minority groups." Cox used his role as part of the educational elite to create a kinship with the justices and to argue that the Court should trust universities to make appropriate admissions decisions without Court intervention. Thus even the oral argument implicitly recognized the existence of small group dynamics: Cox appealed to the justices' sense that he was one of them and that ultimately he was not working at cross-purposes to their best interest.

The opinion of the Court was divided, and Justice Lewis Powell played a pivotal role. Four justices, Burger, Rehnquist, Stevens, and Stewart, interpreting the controversy narrowly, believed that Title VI[14] had been violated by the University's admission policy and that Allan Bakke should be admitted to the medical school.[15]

Justices Brennan, Blackmun, Marshall, and White believed that no equal protection or Title VI violation had occurred and that a race-based classification would not always be per se invalid.[16] These justices would prohibit a race-based classification that was irrelevant or stigmatizing, but they did not view remedying past discrimination as an irrelevant or pernicious use of race. This opinion pointed out that a race-based classification that disadvantaged whites as a group lacked the indicia of suspectness associated with a classification that disadvantaged Blacks. Classifications that disadvantaged whites did not exist in the context of a history of prior discrimination against whites; whites were not a discrete and insular minority; race-based classifications were relevant to remedy past discrimination; and the remedy, here the Davis plan, was crafted to avoid stigma against whites, the group Bakke alleged was hurt.

The Brennan group, rejecting minimum scrutiny equal protection review, articulated a test to review race-based classifications that was based on the "middle-level scrutiny" equal protection review that had been previously articulated in sex-based discrimination cases. First, the articulated purpose of an allegedly remedial racial classification should be reviewed; here the concurring justices said that remedying the effects of past societal discrimination was an acceptable purpose. Second, the Court should review whether the means chosen bore a substantial relation to that articulated purpose. Thus the Brennan group would ask whether the Davis Medical School special admissions program, which set aside sixteen out of one hundred spots for disadvantaged minorities, served an important governmental objective and was substantially related to achievement of that objective.

Powell, writing for the majority, was joined in part of his opinion by both groups of justices. He was the only justice to subscribe to the entire opinion, and his role, weaving a path between the disagreeing camps, enhanced his image as a mediator and facilitator on the Court. In his opinion, Powell rejected the notion of benign discrimination and the notion that there are majorities and minorities. He said that strict scrutiny should apply to all racial classifications and that racial classifications could not be used as a remedy in the absence of a finding of constitutional or statutory discrimination by the appropriate legislative, judicial, or administrative body. This meant that the University could not decide for itself that it needed to remedy societal discrimination in its admissions policy. Powell rejected several of the University's arguments as to why, under strict scrutiny of the race classification, an important government purpose was being served that warranted upholding the classification. He did not find that the need to remedy the deficit of minority doctors, to remedy societal discrimination, or to provide doctors for under-served communities justified sustaining a racial classification.

But Powell did find that the final argument made by the University to support its special admissions program, the need for a diverse student body, was protected by academic freedom under the First Amendment. He concluded that "[t]he freedom of a university to make its own judgments as to education included the selection of its student body." Essentially Powell was telling universities across the nation to be more like Harvard and to use race, if at all, as just one factor in admissions. But the significance of the message, delivered in this guise, is that acting affirmatively is permissible only if one does not do it too openly. Such a message legitimates the notion that it is not quite acceptable to engage in affirmative action, adding to the uneasiness that surrounds the ideal of diversity. And it further suggests that there is a limit to how much affirmative action is allowable. Finally, by grounding this apologetic endorsement of affirmative action in the First Amendment principle of free speech and academic freedom, rather than in the Fourteenth Amendment's guarantee of equal protection of the laws, the Supreme Court obscured the essence of equality at stake in the decision. Diversity, which is essential for equality, is a continuing component of democracy.

The Segregated Reality

Richard Chused reports that "[r]acial tokenism is alive and well at American law schools. About one third of all schools. . . have no Black faculty members. Another third have just one."[17] Chused also documents the "failure of a sizeable segment of law schools, including many of the highest stature, to hire substantial numbers of women." Chused's survey of the 1986-87 academic year showed that women composed 11 percent of tenured classroom faculty.

Chused identifies two excuses offered by racially segregated all-male faculties to justify the lack of racial and gender diversity at their institutions: (1) qualified applicants are unavailable, and (2) a slot or position is not available. Chused's study asserts that both of these excuses are "hollow," because enough faculties have achieved diversity to show that there are qualified candidates for faculty positions, and because turnover is high enough that positions will become available. He advocates that "commitment, devotion of time, willingness to confess error, conscious devotion to finding and using new methods for recruiting faculty, placement of existing women and minority faculty on hiring and tenure committees [, and] the use of substantial numbers of open faculty slots as targets for the fulfillment of openly stated hiring goals" be substituted for these excuses as a means of achieving faculty diversity.

But what happens when there is a position and a "qualified applicant" who is a minority or female? Are other excuses used to keep this person from being appointed to the job?

A Story about Progress

"You just have to be patient, Jessica," said Richard, one of her white liberal faculty colleagues. "Progress is slow at a school this small. We've hired six women and minorities in fifteen years and five white men. They get one spot, we get one spot. Why is that so bad?"

"Maybe you're right in practical terms, Richard. Maybe there is no hope we can do any better. But every one of those slots that has gone to a woman or a minority has led to an appointment only after a fight. Yet these people have all been well qualified according to the very rules establishing qualifications that this institution has traditionally followed. Why the resistance every time? What are people afraid of?"

"Do you really want me to answer that?" asked Richard. Jessica nodded, stubbornly.

"Now, Jessica, you know the unspoken reasons as well as I do," said Richard. "Some people are just worried that they won't be comfortable with a minority or a woman, or they're afraid they might be shown up intellectually, or they're afraid the newcomer will make waves, making this a less comfortable place for them to be."

Jessica didn't think her colleagues were bad or evil people. She just thought they didn't want anyone to rock the boat. She was meeting with Richard to ask for his help concerning the position presently before the faculty. "I'm going to try to get the faculty to hire Teresa Vallero," she said. When Richard shook his head, Jessica bristled.

"What's the matter?"

Teresa Vallero had graduated Phi Beta Kappa from a prestigious national university, Order of the Coif from a top Midwestern law school, been an articles editor of the law review, in which she had published two student notes, clerked for a United States Circuit Court judge, taught for three years at Jefferson, another local law school, and had returned to the practice of law. She had better credentials than many members of the Holmes faculty. She was also a Black-Latina.

Richard shrugged. "It's their turn. If you try to push for her, people will get angry and we'll be undermined on other issues."

Jessica couldn't believe what she was hearing. "I'm going to do this, Richard. Do I have your vote?"

"I won't oppose her," said Richard. "You have my vote, but I'm not going to help you either. I like Teresa, but the last candidate we hired was considered one of us. Some people even opposed his candidacy, saying that because I was on the faculty, we didn't need another person like me. It's not our turn."

A Story about Leadership

Jessica went to the dean to make a plea for leadership from him in the direction of affirmative action.

"You know what I think about affirmative action," said the dean, who had made clear in the past that he did not think much of it.

"Did you see the president's message in the last AALS newsletter?[18] It talked about the need for legal academicians to take affirmative action seriously—to try to integrate the legal profession," Jessica began, but the dean interrupted her.

"I saw it, and if that's what she thinks, it's probably why they have so many problems at UCLA with the bar exam."[19]

Jessica sighed. There was not much point in trying to have a conversation with the dean about this subject. Affirmative action was inextricably linked in his mind with admitting or hiring people with lower qualifications than should be required.

To Jessica, affirmative action meant something quite different. She herself was an affirmative action professor—someone who would not have become a legal educator but for the action of Holmes College, acting affirmatively in seeking her out and asking her to consider joining the faculty.

"No," he told Jessica. "I won't help you convince the faculty to hire Teresa Vallero. I have a different agenda. Besides, I don't think she's very good. I wasn't impressed by her faculty presentation."

"Why not?" asked Jessica. "I thought she was brilliant; she had some important new ideas about equal protection theory."

"I had been looking forward to it. But she wasn't forceful. I just don't have a very good impression of her."

Jessica knew that the dean taught bankruptcy and corporate tax and was not familiar with the equal protection and employment discrimination field. He could not realize the kind of contribution

Teresa's ideas could make to that field; he also did not think that area of law terribly important.

"Besides," the dean continued, "as a faculty, we have argued and fought over affirmative action in both faculty hiring and student admissions. We don't need another fight like that."

In the late 1970s the dean had tried to scrap the special admissions program by which minority and economically disadvantaged students had been admitted to the law school. The faculty split down the middle, amid student demonstrations and alumni outcry. The program had been retained by one vote. Some members of the faculty did not speak to each other for months after this fight. A Black woman lawyer, Josefa Jamison, was hired to direct the academic support program for these admittees. But she was not hired as a faculty member; she did not even have a mailbox in the faculty mail room.

The next big affirmative action fight that divided the faculty was over minority hiring. An African American male candidate was opposed as having no prior teaching experience. An Asian male candidate with teaching experience was opposed as not having produced any legal scholarship. One group believed that "reasons" were always given for dismissing qualified minority candidates. The other group believed that curricular needs at the school were being ignored in the search for affirmative action professors.

Throughout the disagreements, affirmative action had been the policy of the law school, but that had meant different things to different people. "I probably couldn't get this job today," Jessica reflected. "There seems to be less interest in affirmative action now, especially for women of any race."

One Is Not Enough

In *Johnson v. Transportation Agency*,[20] the U.S. Supreme Court upheld against a Title VII challenge a voluntary affirmative action plan that considered the applicant's sex as part of the hiring decision.

The case had originated when a male employee of a county agency claimed he was passed over for promotion because of his sex. The agency, noting that women were underrepresented among agency employees in relation to the county labor force, had adopted a voluntary affirmative action plan that allowed the agency "to consider as one factor the sex of a qualified applicant." Women's advocates hailed the case as a great victory; opponents decried the decision as anti-egalitarian, anti-merit, and pro-quotas.

But the record showed that of 238 skilled craft worker positions, the job classification at issue in this case, not one of those positions was held by a woman. On these facts it would be sex discrimination not to hire a qualified woman for the position. The case is another example of the need for affirmative action to achieve nondiscrimination.

Seven candidates had been eligible for the job at issue in the litigation, a road dispatcher position. Petitioner Johnson had tied for second, and Diane Joyce, the female applicant who was promoted, had been ranked third in the promotion evaluations. Both had been rated "well-qualified."

The Supreme Court opinion by Brennan, joined by Marshall, Blackmun, Powell, and Stevens, upheld the agency's affirmative action plan, commenting with favor that it involved "traditionally segregated job classification[s] in which women have been significantly underrepresented." Furthermore, the plan set aside "no specific number of positions for minorities or women." The plan was temporary and would be used to attain, not maintain, a balanced workforce. Male employees had no absolute entitlement to be promoted to that job; but the plan did not pose an absolute bar either. The Court further commented on the value of voluntary efforts to further the objective of Title VII, which is nondiscrimination. Ironically, in recognizing the "contribution that voluntary employer action can make in eliminating the vestiges of discrimination in the workplace," the Court recognized the very legacy of societal discrimination, the ongoing presence of racism and sexism, that it had declined to acknowledge in the *Bakke* decision.

The *Johnson* decision itself makes a statement in favor of affirmative action—the kind of statement that, if it had been consistently developed, could have been influential in the same way *Brown v. Board of Education* was. But the Court's affirmative action jurisprudence remained stuck at the tokenism level, approving action only when faced with the "inexorable zero,"[21] the total absence of any unprivileged group, in this case women.

A Story about First Women

Jessica telephoned Sandra, a white colleague at a national law school in the East. She described the hiring situation to seek advice. "You know, not only is Teresa Black and Latina, but she's also so tall; she's almost six feet, you know. I think some of the men are intimidated by how powerful she looks. And the combination of her size and color is frightening to them."

"Have you told her to wear flats?" asked Sandra.

"You make this sound like a junior high prom," protested Jessica.

"Well, how different is it really?" was Sandra's grim reply. "If she were applying here, the words of the debate would focus on her scholarship, but that's a very subjective criterion, as you know. Certain things become fashionable and acceptable in scholarship— civic republicanism is big now. Whatever's new or different may be described as 'drivel.'"

"For a bunch of people who pride themselves on being independent thinkers, they're incredibly conformist, aren't they?" mused Jessica.

"Sometimes I think they're more worried about finding someone they can have lunch with," answered Sandra, "and when lunch is at one of their all-male clubs, it *is* a problem fitting us in. I'm getting sick of it, so I'm taking a position against affirmative action at my school."

"What!" Jessica couldn't suppress her disbelief.

"Listen," said Sandra, cutting off the tirade she felt Jessica was about to launch, "when I was hired I was told it was because I was a woman. Now ten years later, after tenure, publishing two books and ten articles, I'm still told that I'm only here because I'm a woman. I'm tired of having to prove myself over and over again. I don't think we should bring women in if they're just going to be perceived as less qualified. We need to hire women and minorities as regular faculty members."

A Story about the Right Woman

Jessica sought refuge by going to talk to Danielle, the third woman who had been hired at Holmes. She was an allied spirit. "You notice these places are never named Thurgood Marshall College of Law or Myra Bradwell Law School," Jessica grumbled in frustration.

"Well, they're not revered the way Holmes was," answered Danielle simply.

"But that's just the point," said Jessica. "That's like saying, 'Why aren't there any great women painters or writers?' Sexism is real. Those designated as stars are so designated by a culture that's predisposed to see certain qualities as important—a certain vision, a certain viewpoint—and is turned off by others. And don't forget what happened to Kirsten. She had been an outstanding Ph.D. student in philosophy, before getting her law degree. When she went to interview with a national law school, the faculty member who interviewed her told her in effect, 'We only hire from the old boy network.' Kirsten had known that, since she'd gotten the interview because one of the 'old boys,' who had been her dissertation adviser, had called and recommended that she be considered. Even coming through the old boy network, she wasn't taken seriously by the interviewers. That school had only three women faculty members out of sixty."

"Well, it's true even stars have trouble finding faculty positions, but Kitty MacKinnon has finally been offered a tenured, full professorship," Danielle said.[22] "Doesn't that make you feel encouraged about the prospects of women law professors? But, the reluctance to hire Teresa here isn't just about discrimination against women. If Jared Daniels were a white woman, politically conservative, our colleague Harold would support her, too."

"So is the problem simply racism?" said Jessica.

"No," Danielle answered slowly, after giving it some thought. "I think it's more complicated—racism and sexism harm women of color more than the sum of the two—or maybe it's racism combined with fear of the F-word, you know, feminism. That's probably why our colleague Gladys likes Jared too. No one could accuse her of being woman-identified. But for Harold, having a conservative woman candidate would be just a convenient excuse, because he would hope others wouldn't support her and then we would have a standoff and hire no one. That's probably what he really wants. He just doesn't want anyone who will disturb the status quo."

"Now I'm really depressed," said Jessica.

"Sorry."

"Well," said Jessica, "at least there's two of us here. But it's amazing that we got here at all. It's like two or three is enough for them, and any more of us would be too scary."

Acting Affirmatively

Without affirmative action, we cannot ensure that our institutions reflect the ideals of equality, fairness, and equal opportunity that are part of our culture. Law professors are not unique in this society in holding divergent views about affirmative action. Law schools, as institutions composed of the individuals within them, are also not unique in society as places where the dominant cultural majority remains in control. Law schools, like other societal institutions, are composed of well-intentioned individuals, who, for the most part, genuinely want to be free of discriminatory attitudes. But as Charles

Lawrence has pointed out in the area of unconscious racism—and his thesis holds for unconscious sexism or heterosexism as well—many acts done with the best intentions are still racist, sexist, or heterosexist not because we are bad people, but because we are products of the society in which we live. Thus, the cycle of exclusion is unwittingly continued.

Four objections are usually raised about affirmative action: (1) it violates the democratic ideal that mandates disregard of color, sex, or sexual orientation; (2) it undermines merit-based selection; (3) it is unfair to those who have not discriminated; and (4) it stigmatizes those it purports to assist. Each argument fails as a reason not to act affirmatively.

Opponents of affirmative action often argue that attention to the race or sex of an applicant reduces an individual to a single attribute, skin color, or sex, and that this process is the antithesis of equal opportunity. This argument is often voiced as, "I don't care if she's blue or green and from Mars, as long as she's competent." The point being made is that race or sex is irrelevant or should be.

One could imagine a society in which race and sex are irrelevant. In such a society we might or might not remember the race or sex of those we meet. But, as Richard Wasserstrom has pointed out, that imagined culture is not this culture.[23] To say that today's world functions that way is to deny reality.

The race-and-sex-are-irrelevant argument is attractive because its proponents advance it as if it were not an ideal, but reality. We are asked to believe that the discrimination-free society is here and that to pay attention to race or sex would be to turn back the clock to the days before racism and sexism were eliminated. A moment's reflection makes it clear that we do not live in such a world. The argument is based on an attractive but false premise, that the nondiscriminatory future is now and that except for the occasional aberrant bigot or sexist, we live in a race- and sex-neutral society.

The second argument made against affirmative action is related to the myth of meritocracy and the fear that affirmative action will result in a lowering of so-called standards. According to this argument, finding qualified women or minorities is difficult or impossible, and standards must be maintained. To the extent that affirmative action retains the meaning of giving special treatment on account of race or sex, opposition to affirmative action is powerfully ingrained in the mainstream of our culture. None of us want that special treatment; we want to be judged on our so-called merit.

Consider this riddle:

> A father and his son were driving to a ball game when their car stalled on the railroad tracks. In the distance a train whistle blew a warning. Frantically, the father tried to start the engine, but in his panic, he couldn't turn the key, and the car was hit by the oncoming train. An ambulance sped to the scene and picked them up. On the way to the hospital, the father died. The son was still alive, but his condition was very serious, and he needed immediate surgery. The moment they arrived at the hospital, he was wheeled into an emergency operating room, and the surgeon came in expecting a routine case. However, on seeing the boy, the surgeon blanched and muttered, "I can't operate on this boy—he's my son."[24]

How could this be? The answer is that the surgeon is the boy's mother. Although this is an obvious answer once the listener thinks about it, the point is that most people do not think about it or else they solve the riddle only after careful thinking. Most people's instantaneous reaction is to picture the surgeon as male.[25]

This riddle reveals societal default assumptions about merit— automatic, unconscious assumptions that channel our thoughts. Members of this culture have trouble seeing white women and minority group members as surgeons, lawyers, senior vice presidents, and law professors: the images society unconsciously associates with these words are male and white. The knowledge that white women and people of color can be surgeons does not help listeners solve the riddle, because the mind makes the culturally accustomed leaps without going through a rational thought process.[26] Present definitions of merit are context-based and shaped by default assumptions.

As to the unfairness affirmative action perpetuates toward those who did not discriminate, consider that we as a society pay for much that we did not personally do. Congress assisted Chrysler, even though all citizens did not mismanage the company. The societal good of inclusion of all its members is most pressing and warrants societal prioritization.

As for stigma, the stigma of being a woman or man-of-color law professor comes from society's default assumptions—a woman in front of the room does not look like Professor Kingsfield in *The Paper Chase*—and not from the existence of affirmative action. Affirmative action should be viewed in a positive light.

A Story about Exclusion

Jessica went to the meeting of her local feminist critical legal theory group.[27] The women were from a range of law schools. Yvonne was one of two tenured women at a nationally known state law school. She had been one of the first women law professors hired nationally. Constance had been the first woman hired at her nationally known private law school. She had two tenured female colleagues. One of them, Virginia, was also present. Jessica and her colleague Danielle, from Holmes, were part of the group, as were Rita, Sheryl, and Ali, who all taught at regionally known state law schools. Sheryl was a Black woman who spoke infrequently in group meetings; she did not have tenure. She was the only woman of color in the group. Rita was an "out" lesbian, who had recently entered law teaching from a successful civil rights practice.

"Eight of us, from five different law schools—it's really appalling—there are ten women on the UCLA faculty alone, and they have a woman dean," said Jessica.

"Well, Jessica, that's not really a fair way to count," responded Virginia. "After all, all of us have at least one woman colleague who is not here. Not all women law professors are interested in feminist legal theory, just because they are women."

"I know that," replied Jessica, with an edge of annoyance in her voice. "But we don't all have nine female colleagues who aren't here. That's my point, and it's remarkable that we have all made it this far in legal academia."

Ali, in whose house they were meeting, asked Danielle, "So how is it going with Teresa? Might you get her?"

"Jessica knows more about that than I do," Danielle replied. "I've been on leave, so I'm not involved in the politics."

Ali turned to Jessica. "So, how does it look?" Ali was interested in hiring and tenure decisions because during her own tenure case, some faculty had objected to her work in feminist jurisprudence. They had told her that her work did not help them understand or deal with the women in their own lives, as if making their lives more comfortable were the goal of feminist jurisprudence.

Jessica said, "You know how it is; there's always a reason that the person isn't good enough. Teresa has all the paper credentials they ever asked for. But so did our last minority candidate. When we pointed out that he met all their previously articulated qualifications, they said he needed to have published. Then he did publish, and they said he needed prior teaching experience. Well, Teresa has met all those conditions, although her publications were both done when she was a student."

"So what's the problem?" asked Constance.

"Now they're saying there is no position—that we can't afford another faculty hire. But you don't have that issue at your school. I heard you have lots of positions. How is your hiring going?"

"I'd like to see us make an offer to Rochelle Adams. She's a fabulous teacher in a business field, where they're always moaning that it's hard to find women. But now they're making an issue of her writing, even though the high quality of her publications was originally the reason she was offered the visit."

"That's used a lot," said Yvonne. "Did you hear what happened to Belinda Fielding? Do you know her? She has been teaching for over fifteen years. She's published lots of articles and a casebook. She's a frequent speaker at AALS panels. When she visited another school in her state university system, the dean told her the visit had been very successful, but that when her writing had been read in the past, people hadn't liked it."

"Well Robert Davis was told the same thing," offered Constance, "after he visited at Harvard and Yale—that he was a great teacher, but he hadn't written 'the kind of article' that would show he was of the caliber to be at that school."

"Are you saying this is not discrimination, because it happens to men, too? Robert is Black, you know," Sheryl interjected.

"No, I know another yardstick seems to be used when women or people of color are measured. But this process—whether hiring or tenure—doesn't seem pleasurable for our white, male colleagues who are subjected to it, either. It's not nurturing, supportive, or a piece of cake for them," Constance replied.

"I can see that," Ali said, "but they still overwhelmingly have the jobs, while women and people of color do not. Look around you— you see bright young white men being hired regularly. But we still have to fight over entry-level positions for young women or minority candidates, and even for lateral hires, for that matter. In fact, I think there may be even greater resistance to lateral hires. And we're being denied tenure at a higher rate, too. The point is that any hire outside the white, male norm is still controversial, subjected to greater scrutiny, and just plain doesn't happen without a lot of pushing within the institutional framework."

Jessica said, "That's the problem with discrimination. It's lose-lose. If you've published a lot, then you're over the hill and don't have anything good left. If you haven't published, then it's not acceptable because you haven't shown you can produce the 'kind of article' valued by that institution. It's another way of saying the candidate doesn't have 'the right stuff.' There's always a reason, by which I mean no real reason at all."

"That happened to a friend of mine," said Virginia. "She was asked to visit at a school on the strength of her writing. The school had a policy of not considering visitors for permanent appointments, which they decided to waive in her case. Then they decided her writing wasn't good enough to earn her the appointment."

"That doesn't even make any sense," said Danielle.

"I forgot to say that between the beginning and end of the process, the school had hired two other women."

"Three's dangerous, right?" Danielle laughed, shaking her head incredulously.

"Did you follow the discrimination case at Boalt Hall?" asked Rita. "Eleanor Swift, who was denied tenure, filed a grievance, claiming sex discrimination. Marge Shultz was given tenure, years after it had been denied to her, after Eleanor filed discrimination charges,[28] and students have been sitting-in in the dean's office and getting arrested. I think they're called the Coalition for a Diversified Faculty."

"Do they make house calls?" asked Danielle.

"Now there would be a thriving business—there's a lot of need," said Virginia.

Sheryl burst out, "I'm sick of this, story after story of exclusion. We as a group do the same thing you're accusing them of. Just look at the dynamics here. This group is dominated by women from the 'fanciest' law schools, all of whom happen to be white."

The group lapsed into an uncomfortable silence, which seemed to be an acknowledgment that Sheryl was right.

Finally Yvonne said, "Until law schools are more diverse, how can a group of women law professors have more minority members? We operate in the existing law school cultural context. It's hard to change the values in that culture and the way it offers its rewards."

"But isn't that what we're asking them to do?" asked Sheryl quietly. Again the silence suggested agreement.

"But aren't we different?" ventured Ali. "At least we're open to talking about it."

"That's a small difference. Talk is cheap," was Sheryl's reply.

"What are you talking about?—we would hire women of all races and male minority law professors." Virginia sounded exasperated.

"But which ones? This group reflects the same elitism, racism, and heterosexism that is part of the legal education hierarchy. Sexism just recedes in importance here because we're all women. You aren't really trying to bring more women of color into *this* group. If you were serious about including more women of color here you would recruit some promising law students or practioners," answered Sheryl.

"I don't understand. We value you as part of the group," Constance reassured her.

"And the professorial majority would say they don't discriminate either," Sheryl replied. "I'm not talking about conscious desire on your part—or on most of theirs. But it will take more than just good intentions to change things—that's what we always tell them."

"I still don't understand," said Virginia. "Is this the battle over what 'qualified' means?—the problem of what is merit? How do you evaluate quality and how do you know when some other dynamic is at work—one we don't even acknowledge?"

Rita said, "Let me tell you a story. A friend of mine was at a faculty meeting where the group discussed writing letters of condolence to the families of two city officials who had been slain. One of the officials was gay.

"The faculty at this meeting voted to send a letter of consolation to the widow of the straight official, but not to the lover of the deceased gay man. A discussion took place at the meeting about why it made sense to make this distinction because the straight man had been an alumnus of the law school, while the gay official was not a lawyer. There were some 'jokes' about what kind of family this gay politician had. The faculty minutes about the meeting made no mention of the discussion, even though a motion had been made and seconded to send a letter to the gay man's family. Three lines in the minutes had been whited out before they were circulated for faculty approval.

"This is how it is: the discussion exists on one level with words about it in apparently neutral language. This is the text. But there is really something else going on. There exists a whole level, beyond the words, where people make decisions and take actions of exclusion. That's the subtext, and it's never talked about. If it becomes visible, it's made invisible—here by Wite-Out—what a great name for it. That's true in this group."

"And it's true," said Jessica, "with my efforts to hire Teresa Vallero."

A Story about Personal Power and Change

"I'm still confused about the 'whole role of sex' in this hiring problem," said Jessica, as the group was finishing its meeting. "The law is not about sex, but there's something like sexual chemistry at work here."

"What does sex have to do with this?" Danielle said. "Are you talking about sexual harassment? In all my years as a professor I have never experienced a male colleague making any insinuation whatsoever."

"Wait a minute," said Rita, "the child abuse statistics alone indicate that at least 30 percent of women are sexually abused. I bet the sexual harassment statistics, if we had accurate ones, would be equally mind-boggling. I just read that 25 percent of California women lawyers surveyed said they had been subjected to sexual harassment in the profession, 11 percent of them on their current jobs."

"One thing at least this group should be able to agree on," Jessica said. "Sexual subordination exists in this culture and women are at risk in this area—but that's not what I'm talking about, really."

"My therapist is an Asian woman who was raised as a Catholic and married a Jewish man, and so she has crossed many cultures," Ali said. "She's fond of pointing out that Western culture doesn't have the last word or even an explanation for all things.[29] In fact, we have no words for some things that are very important. The Hindus call the physical energy Kundalini; Buddhism has another set of names. It's the energy that flows from the pelvic base, up and out."

"Are you talking about sexual energy?" Yvonne asked.

"Yes and no," said Jessica. "This feeling may be confused with sexual energy, but it's more than that—it's the power you're exerting when you speak to a roomful of ninety people."[30]

"I think it's why male faculty have such a hard time around us. As men, they're used to responding to that female energy as sexual, or else as someone who has been their mother and nurturant, or their daughter. At least for our older colleagues, they haven't experienced women in many other ways, and so they're confused about how to relate to us. We *feel* different to them; just like a roomful of them feels different to us."

"This whole conversation is making me feel weird," said Virginia.

"I agree," Jessica responded . "It's impossible to talk about this stuff without sounding like a New Age hippie freak."

"Or even worse, a Californian," smiled Constance.

"But think about the feeling inside you, not just sexually, but whenever you take charge of a class or commune with a hard-to-write paragraph, when you're really in touch with your own personal power," Jessica said.

"Like when you get a sick child to take her medicine," offered Sheryl.

"And think," continued Jessica, "that we women in Western culture don't even have a name for that. It's so powerful that we aren't even permitted to name it. It says something about the importance of this thing to the power of patriarchy that it has taken away our ability to name it—it must be very significant."

"What does all this have to do with the problem of getting women hired at law schools?" asked Danielle.

"Don't you see—the dynamics of personal interaction and group interaction have as much to do with this whole hiring problem as any law," answered Rita.

"Are you saying that law is pointless?" asked Yvonne.

"No," said Rita, "it means that law can serve as a model for behavior. For example, integration should be an ideal, not segregation. But the status quo will just keep rolling on. Their sense of *our* differentness is why they will keep us out, without their necessarily realizing that this is what they are doing. They are just instinctively looking for more of the same."

Moving toward Diversity

The obstacles encountered in moving toward diversity on any faculty at any historic point cannot be underestimated. No body of case law on affirmative action can change the group dynamics, institutional and personal, that control the hiring and tenure decisions. Nonetheless, law plays an important ideological role in our society, nurturing our aspirations toward justice. These group dynamics are played out in the shadow of the law and what it teaches society about affirmative action. Legal decisions could play an important role in achieving diversity, much as *Brown v. Board of Education* and the

John Minor Wisdom desegregation cases that followed it set the tone for working toward integration in the 1950s and 1960s.

As a faculty member faced with one of these "discussions" about hiring, what can you do to facilitate the achievement of diversity? It is important to recognize that this is a political process and not to allow yourself to be silenced. A form of silencing occurs in these discussions concerning faculty hiring because we are denied the use of words to describe what is really going on. Even efforts to name the discrimination and privileging we see in the cycle of exclusion often fall on unresponsive ears.

Jessica recalled trying to identify sex discrimination as an issue to one colleague who replied, "You really have a chip on your shoulder about sex. You see sexism in everything."

"You think I have a chip on my shoulder about sex? You should talk to some of my friends," was all Jessica could muster in response.

But Jessica had been told to be careful about identifying sexism as an issue in that colleague's presence. He did not want to hear about it. So Jessica has to be able to talk about sexism in some other way, with some other words, or not at all. Yet the words we use are important, framing the conceptualization of the debate. That is why this chapter has sought to reclaim the notion of acting affirmatively. And that is why this chapter has told stories. Allegations of sexism, or any other ism, are not very persuasive; but examples from people's lives are. Telling the stories of the pain caused by the micro- and macro-aggressions that result from failing to yield to the dominant cultural norms can give new words to the discussion. Stories can show the preferences that have been unspoken.

Stories can be told about those outside the dominant cultural majority using their personal power and building coalitions with others to effect changes in legal education. Nationally, the founding of the Gay and Lesbian Legal Issues Section within the AALS is one such story. The passage of AALS bylaws amendments providing for affirmative action and nondiscrimination is another. Changes can happen within particular institutions if individual members raise the dynamics to a level of consciousness and discuss them. Consciousness-raising is a first step toward change. We owe it to ourselves to proceed so that the other steps can unfold.

The notion of law as ideology or as a psychological phenomenon is particularly important in the area of affirmative action as it relates to law teaching. As members of law faculties, we are doing more than teaching a body of "rules and penalties laid down by agencies of government in order to effectuate their will."[31] We, the teachers of law, influence the consciousness of law that our students, as well as others in society, will have. The legal academy has an opportunity to exemplify diversity in point of view and leadership in achieving nondiscrimination.

The confusion about the meanings of affirmative action reflect the ambivalence in the culture, in our collective law-consciousness, and among the colleagues at institutions like Holmes Law School about the meaning of nondiscrimination. What will happen to Teresa Vallero? Will she be hired? We in legal education can write the ending to this story and to the many stories like it. If we do nothing, the status quo or institutional rules as they exist will operate, and most likely she will not be hired. But we can try to change that norm.

The challenge of the 1990s and the twenty-first century is to create a legal system that is just, in the sense of treating like situations alike, yet that also is responsive to the diverse social realities, the cultural differences, reflected in modern American life. The law must include us all, or it will not be relevant to the entire community. In this search we can start with ourselves—the teachers of law. Because we train the members of the profession, we can effect change by examining our admissions and hiring practices. There is no place like home to start.

Chapter 7

Stephanie M. Wildman

The Quest for Justice
The Rule of Law and Invisible Systems of Privilege

Introduction: The Aspiration for Justice

In the administration and teaching of law today, the role of justice remains highly ambiguous. If a judge cites justice in support of her opinion, lawyers and litigants (especially those who do not like the result) accuse her of rationalization or—worse—groping for a reason for the outcome. Those critics suggest that more objective standards such as statutes, case law, or economic doctrine should determine outcomes. Law students, even law teachers, see law school as having relegated consideration of justice to the back burner, compartmentalizing it into intellectual courses about jurisprudence. In a commencement speech last year, one of our graduates explained that a friend had asked what she had learned during three years in law school. When the graduate mentioned torts, contracts, and criminal law, her friend responded, "But where is the class about justice?"

To the vast majority of Americans today, the idea of justice remains deeply alluring. Because we aspire to justice, we feel we are a community of moral beings, even as the bonds of society crumble around us. But lawyers and laypersons alike frequently conflate the idea of justice and the concept of the rule of law, believing that the application of the rule of law will produce justice. Thus lawyers and others view the rule of law (including justice as its presumed by-product) as the underpinning of societal legitimacy. The notion of the rule of law is fundamental to United States culture, to its sense of self as a nation, and to its sense of self as law-abiding.

Thus the U.S. legal system aspires to achieve the rule of law and the just results that presumably flow from it. The rule of law in turn embodies the idea of fair and equal treatment—treating like cases alike and all individuals equally. These aspirations to fairness and equality suggest that our collective subconscious harbors a genuine desire to end oppression and subordination throughout society. But, as the affirmative action discussion shows, when we apply legal standards of equal treatment to a social and economic culture that systematically privileges some and disadvantages others, the result is the maintenance of an uneven and unequal status quo. One person's equality may be another's oppression, because of the perpetuation of existing systems of privilege and power. The failure to recognize and discuss these systems results in their continuation.

The law, as such, no longer overtly endorses or intentionally sustains the systems of privilege that exist in our society. Yet legal values like justice and equality obscure the presence of these systems, which are based on sex, race, sexual orientation, and class. The United States is a white supremacist culture, which privileges people with white skin over racial and ethnic minorities. U.S. culture is patriarchal, meaning that men and male-associated attributes are valued, while women and female-associated attributes are not. Patriarchy also privileges heterosexual behavior over gay or lesbian sexuality. The culture denies the existence of social classes, yet money means access not only to luxuries, but also to basic human needs such as food, clothing, shelter, and medical care. These individual systems create an intertwined system of privilege and subordination.

Religion is another component of culture. Religious belief interacts with these systems of privilege. The struggle for religious freedom has lasted throughout history and continues today. The First Amendment's separation of religion and government represents this country's response to that struggle. Through that amendment our constitutional law seeks to protect religious freedom and keep the religious realm separated from the state. Thus our social system is not supposed to privilege organized religion or religious belief over the secular realm. But this protection of the secular creates a peculiar vacuum, in which religion is supposed to be invisible, yet Christmas is a national holiday. Even the phrasing "church [but not synagogue or mosque] and state" privileges Christianity as the defining religion for constitutional drafting.

Systems of privilege and the religious/secular dichotomy intertwine with the rule of law to contribute to the undermining of justice. Systemic privileging and oppression remain invisible and undiscussed, in accordance with the unwritten rules of our society. The rule of law does nothing to end this invisibility and may even contribute to its continuation. Thus the very act of seeing that the rule of law and systems of privilege undermine justice is itself problematic. A full attack on privileging and oppression can begin in earnest only when the legal profession recognizes this privileging dynamic. But this reality—privilege—that we must see has not even found articulation in legal vocabulary.

Faced with the failure of law to see or address privilege, legal commentators have increasingly turned to literature, particularly drama. Literature directly addresses the relationship between justice and the rule of law on the one hand and privileging and oppression on the other.[1] The viewers of a theatrical performance participate in the experience and range of emotions in a unique way that enables them to feel the injustice that results from privilege. Justice and injustice are the stuff of drama. Trials, the stage on which modern-day dramas of justice are enacted, have been likened to theater. With the rise of Court TV, the live theater of the courtroom is beamed into many homes. Through the lens of theater, the aspirational value of justice is reinvented and the conflicts created between that aspiration and the rule of law and systems of privilege become possible to see.

This chapter reconsiders the role of the rule of law in relation to the aspiration for justice and examines the role of law and justice in three plays. Shakespeare's *Merchant of Venice* exemplifies a dominant cultural view[2] of racism and anti-Semitism: the rule of law, a product of the dominant culture, plays a heroic role in relation to these isms. In Arthur Miller's play *A View from the Bridge*, law is the bridge between the European Old World and the new American culture. But again the law represents a dominant culture of assimilation, leaving racial minorities, white women, gays, and lesbians out of the dream. The tension between the rule of law, the need to be fair, and the perpetuation of systems of privilege becomes apparent in Anna Deavere Smith's *Fires in the Mirror*. Until the dominant cultural blindness to these systems and their relation to the rule of law changes, the aspiration for justice and fairness in the rule of law will remain simply a myth.

The Rule of Law: Its Relation to Justice and Its Role in Perpetuating Oppression

The judge is one of the great cultural icons of the Western world. The Western image of the wise judge began as early as the biblical tale of

Solomon, who says he will cut the baby in half to determine its true mother. Wisdom is the hallmark of the great judge, who both follows the law and dispenses justice.

The cultural aspiration unites law and justice, yet the ideas of law and justice do not always peacefully coexist. The rule of law, an idea first articulated as "a rule of law, not of men,"[3] originally meant fairness—following rules rather than allowing blatant exercise of power by a ruler. Justice could mean clemency by those in power or an exercise of power to achieve a fair result.

Thus a tension between the rule of law and an aspiration for justice did exist. That tension was captured in the modern era by the musical *Camelot*, when King Arthur must decide whether to follow the letter of the law and kill the queen for treason or to follow his heart and let her live.[4]

Yet the rule of law remains equivalent to justice in the minds of some. To act according to the rule of law, and implicitly justice and fairness, means to treat a dispute in the same manner as prior disputes have been handled. Equal treatment seems like the epitome of fairness, until we look closer. An evaluation of same treatment has generally meant that some parties were defined as part of the community and others as outsiders. Receiving the same treatment, while still remaining defined as an outsider, does nothing to change the existing power relations and the privileging of insider status.

Critical legal scholars have debated the meaning of the rule of law, declaring the rule of law to be infinitely manipulable and therefore not a rule at all.[5] Rather, they assert, the rule of law is political and it reinforces existing power.

The British historian E. P. Thompson has described the rule of law as reinforcing and legitimating existing class relations.[6] But he has also defended the rule of law, pointing out that the law does more than impose class power. Thompson describes people as "not as stupid" as some think. "They will not be mystified by the first man who puts on a wig." He continues,

> The essential precondition for the effectiveness of law, in its function as ideology, is that it shall display an independence from gross manipulation and shall seem to be just. It cannot seem to be so without upholding its own logic and criteria of equity; indeed, on occasion, by actually being just.[7]

For Thompson being just "on occasion" is important; in a sense it is the best we can expect from the rule of law.

Thompson concludes that

> There is a difference between arbitrary power and the rule of law. We ought to expose the shams and inequities which may be concealed beneath this law. But the rule of law itself, the imposing of effective inhibitions upon power and the defence of the citizen from power's all-intrusive claims, seems to me to be an unqualified human good. To deny or belittle this good is, in this dangerous century when the resources and pretensions of power continue to enlarge, a desperate error of intellectual abstraction.[8]

Morton Horwitz professes shock at Thompson's characterization of the rule of law as "an unqualified human good." Horwitz comments that the rule of law "undoubtedly restrains power, but it also prevents power's benevolent exercise." He explains,

> It creates formal equality—a not inconsiderable virtue—but it promotes substantive inequality by creating a consciousness that radically separates law from politics, means from ends, processes from outcomes. By promoting procedural justice it

enables the shrewd, the calculating, and the wealthy to manip-
ulate its forms to their own advantage. And it ratifies and legitimates an adversarial, competitive, and atomistic conception of
human relations.[9]

The Horwitz critique is representative of recent critical legal scholarship.

Thompson is not the only one defending the rule of law. Legal
scholars of color have differed with the critical legal scholars' view
that rights are illusory. Rights made alchemically out of nothing,
they contend, have forged for racial minorities in this country a vehicle with which to argue and urge that the rule of law be just.

In one well-known example, Patricia Williams compares her experience of apartment hunting in New York City with Peter Gabel's.
Both wanted to build trust and relationships with the people in
whose houses they would be living. But their methods were quite different, reflecting the privileging of whiteness and maleness in society.
Gabel, to counteract his white, male authority and to establish inti-
macy, exchanged $900 in cash for a promise and a handshake.
Williams, African American and female, signed "a detailed, lengthily
negotiated, finely printed lease . . . [establishing herself] as the ideal
arm's-length transactor."[10] The idea of rules that could be followed
by both parties was reassuring to Williams to establish her presence
as an equal in the transaction for the other party, who might not
view her that way.

Insight into the operation of the rule of law is also provided by
Lynne Henderson, who comments that there is a "cultural assumption that the Rule of Law automatically prevents tyranny and oppression."[11] But as Henderson points out, "Even the prime virtue of the
Rule of Law, that all are bound by it, does not dictate the *content* of
the law."[12] Henderson's essay points out that the rule of law lacks substance and that simply following rules can lead to authoritarianism.[13]

> Substantive authoritarianism means opposition to the "liberal" values of tolerance of ambiguity and difference, insistence on obedience to rules, insistence on conformity, and use of coercion and punishment to ensure that obedience. . . . Substantive authoritarianism oppresses in the name of order and control.[14]

Henderson concludes that substantive authoritarianism flourishes when we cease to take personal responsibility for the suffering and oppression of others in the name of obedience to authority, including legal authority.

The rule of law can operate in conjunction with justice only where its substantive content is codified. As I have explained earlier, interlocking invisible systems of privilege operate in our culture. Only when we discuss what has been invisible can any movement toward justice occur. Examining privilege is a way to make these power systems visible. The rule of law has focused on discriminatory, differential treatment, not on privilege. As a result these systems remain.

Is it possible to codify justice into a rule of law? The rule of law already mandates equal opportunity, a cultural acknowledgment of the need for diversity and inclusive community. That mandate, however, cannot become a reality while invisible systems of privilege exist. Laws are still subject to interpretation by people. The need for analysis, application, and explanation results in a cultural interpretation constructed by people who have the privilege to do it.

The inclusion of everyone in societal decision making needs to be named as a goal. We must make visible the systems of privilege that exclude, and we must examine the role of the rule of law in maintaining those systems. Naming and telling the truth are fundamental parts of recovery programs, which are based on honesty.

Perhaps we need a recovery program for the rule of law to help it become aligned with the aspiration for justice. Plays provide a kind of permission for honesty, presenting a view of culture and the role of law and justice within that culture. Even *The Merchant of Venice*, much criticized as anti-Semitic for its portrayal of Shylock, shows his humanity and pain at exclusion and forced conformity. Anna Deavere Smith's work takes honesty to new heights; she uses real people's actual words from her interviews with them in her portrayal of their characters. Theater provides us with a lens to examine the social order with honesty.

The Plays: Theater as a Lens to Examine the Social Order

Walter Cohen, examining the similarity in sixteenth- and seventeenth-century English and Spanish theater, observed, "Both the plays and their theaters depended on the larger cultural, political, and social contours of the age."[15] Cohen asserts that the nature of the English and Spanish political states fostered the theater and accounted for the parallels between the two dramatic traditions.[16] Just as the plays depended on that cultural, political, and social context, a study of the plays reveals much about that context and provides insight into the role of law within that social framework.

The Merchant of Venice reflects the English origins of the American legal system. *A View from the Bridge* and *Fires in the Mirror* provide vehicles for examining the aspiration for justice in contemporary society.

A. The Merchant of Venice

The Merchant of Venice is probably best remembered as a play about Portia, Shylock, and their battle over the meaning of law. Portia's suitor, Bassanio, is also a significant character. Yet the play is named for Antonio, who is the merchant of the title.

Antonio, initially forlorn, cheers up with the arrival of Bassanio. Some modern productions make clear that Antonio's sadness results from his unrequited love for Bassanio.[17] The playwright then introduces Portia as "a lady richly left." Bassanio's interest in Portia appears to be almost entirely mercenary.

Portia's father's will requires that her suitor pick one of three caskets, made from gold, silver, and lead. The suitor who picks the correct casket wins the right to marry Portia. Although Portia says she cannot choose or refuse a suitor,[18] she seems to know more about the caskets than she admits. She tells her servant to "set a deep glass of Rhenish wine on the contrary casket," of a suitor she despises.

Meanwhile, Bassanio has been meeting with Shylock, the Jewish moneylender, referred to in Shakespeare's list of dramatis personae as "a Jew." Shylock is about to agree to loan Bassanio three thousand ducats on Antonio's bond. Shylock asks to speak with Antonio. Bassanio replies, "If it please you to dine with us."

Shylock answers, "I will not eat with you, drink with you, nor pray with you." Shylock explains that he hates Antonio because he is a Christian and because he lends money free of interest. But we learn that Antonio hates Jewish people and Shylock as well.[19] Shylock tells Antonio, "You call me misbeliever, cutthroat dog, and spet upon my Jewish gaberdine." Yet Shylock says, "I would be friends with you, and have your love." It seems that he wants to loan the money on Antonio's promise of repayment, without charging the interest that has caused him to be reviled. Antonio and Shylock agree to the loan on condition that Antonio will forfeit a pound of flesh if he fails in repayment. At this point it seems clear that Shylock intends no bodily harm;[20] rather, he makes this offer as an effort of friendship, connection, and acceptance.

Meanwhile the Prince of Morocco, usually played by a dark-skinned actor, arrives to woo Portia. He chooses the gold casket, finding a head of death inside. He departs, and Portia says, "A gentle riddance. Draw the curtains, go. Let all of his complexion choose me so."[21]

Jessica, Shylock's daughter, aspires to marry Bassanio's friend Lorenzo and become a Christian and "loving wife." Jessica dresses as a boy and runs off with Lorenzo, carrying her father's fortune. When Shylock learns his daughter has fled, his cry is "Justice! The Law!"[22]

Bassanio picks the correct casket, winning Portia, and learns that Antonio has lost all his ships. Shylock, furious at his daughter's running away, insists on collecting his pound of flesh. In his insistence he relies on justice, saying, "The Duke shall grant me justice."

Some of Antonio's friends console him, saying that the duke will not grant this kind of forfeiture. But Antonio explains, "The Duke cannot deny the course of law," because Venice depends on trade with all nations. Faith in law is the glue that holds the international transactions together.

In the famous court scene, Shylock continues to rely on the law, which he believes equals justice, as each character in turn pleads with him to be merciful. Shylock insists, "I stand here for law." Portia, dressed as Balthasar, a doctor of laws, enters the court. She also urges Shylock to be merciful, explaining that mercy cannot be compelled and that "in the course of justice, none of us should see salvation."[23] She too conflates justice with following the rule of law.

Portia agrees that the bond is forfeit, urging Shylock yet again, "Be merciful. Take thrice thy money; bid me tear the bond." But Shylock remains adamant that "by the law" he will proceed to judgment. Portia then tells him he can cut the pound of flesh, but "no jot of blood." Shylock, in relying on the letter of the law, is stuck with a bond he cannot collect. Furthermore, he has violated another law of Venice by seeking the life of a citizen. The penalty for this violation is that his life lies in the hands of the duke. Thus Shylock, who would show no mercy, must rely on the duke's mercy, which is granted before it is even sought. Half of Shylock's possessions are forfeit to Antonio and half to the state. The duke also requires, at Antonio's suggestion, that Shylock become a Christian.

The Merchant of Venice symbolizes the triumph of justice over the letter of the law. But the triumph of this justice marks the undoing of Shylock. It is not enough that he forfeits his bond and wealth; he is told he must become a Christian. His daughter's forsaking him, running off with a Christian man and taking Shylock's money, is approved by this version of justice. Thus *The Merchant of Venice* represents a dominant cultural view of justice; it salutes the triumph of the dominant culture and the assimilation of the other.

But even within that vision of dominant cultural triumph, the cost of assimilation is shown, if one looks for it. The dominant culture fosters heterosexuality, sexism, and racism. Nothing in the triumph of justice alters that status quo or even challenges it. Shylock, as an individual, challenges anti-Semitism and is crushed by the power of law. Portia challenges sexism, but only indirectly by pretending to be other than herself.

Antonio is a very melancholy character, although he is happy to help his friend Bassanio. As noted earlier, some productions of the play have hinted that Antonio himself is in love with Bassanio and that the reason for his melancholy is the heterosexism of society, which bars the expression of that love. Based as it is on Bassanio's quest to marry Portia, the play certainly fosters heterosexist assumptions about the proper ordering of human relations.

Scenes with Portia and her suitors provide the only mention of race in the play. The default assumption is whiteness; Portia makes her preference of whiteness explicit. Even though she holds this view, Portia's name has become associated with a female vision of justice. But even she must dress like a man to enter the world in which justice between Shylock and Antonio is to be determined.

Her justice is celebrated as a justice of mercy, a triumph of the spirit—not the letter—of the law. But what kind of justice is this for Shylock? It is a justice of the dominant culture, to which he is commanded to assimilate, just as Portia had to assimilate into it to perform the judicial role. She could not represent justice as herself, a woman. We are all one, but the one is the dominant culture, here Christian and male.

The story line of *The Merchant of Venice* is well known. But reducing the story to its "facts" in this manner, stripped of Shakespeare's language and nuance, and indeed stripped of the power of the dramatic production itself, renders it lifeless and drains away its emotional power. Summaries of facts in appellate cases similarly drain the real-life situation of its force as the legal language appropriates the reality, twisting it to fit its own view of the world.

The emotion is present in Shakespeare's text and palpable in the theater as the play unfolds. The emotion pulses through the audience as it watches the anti-Semitism, the racism, the titillating excitement when the women, dressed as men to enter the world and fool their lovers, first appear. In some productions, Antonio's love for Bassanio is a locus for emotion and mourning over that forbidden love. This emotion makes possible an awareness of systems of privilege and subordination.

In *The Merchant of Venice* the poverty of the letter of the law, blind adoration of the rule, is revealed. Justice is achieved by letting the merchant Antonio live and by not letting Shylock take his pound of flesh. But what of justice for the Jew? For him justice was fulfilling the bond, even at the cost of life, to show he was an equal under law. His punishment, becoming a Christian, erases him and ignores the context of hatred that has motivated his desire.

When we examine the play we see women in the public sphere, recognized by law only when they act like men, silence on the question of race, silence as to sexual orientation, and anti-Semitism resolved by assimilation. "Act like me or be silent." The dominant cultural message states that law seems irrelevant at best or an assistant in the process at worst. Can law do better?

B. A View from the Bridge

In Arthur Miller's play *A View from the Bridge*,[24] the narrator, Alfieri, is a lawyer. He introduces the audience to the working-class Brooklyn neighborhood where the action takes place by commenting on the uneasy greeting he gets from his neighbors. "[T]o meet a lawyer or a priest on the street is unlucky." Alfieri believes that his neighbors' suspicion comes from the link between lawyers and law. Law has not been a friendly idea to these Sicilian immigrants, but "[j]ustice is very important." The community regard for Alfieri reflects the tension between the meaning of rules, used for authoritarian control, and perceptions in the community about justice.

In this introduction, Miller establishes the link between lawyers and the symbolism of law, but he also suggests that law may be separate from justice. The image of justice that Alfieri invokes is the powerlessness of lawyers and implicitly law when some trouble is set to "run its bloody course."

Eddie, a longshore worker, lives with Beatrice, his wife, and Catherine, the daughter of Beatrice's sister, who died. Eddie and Beatrice have raised Catherine, who is now seventeen and about to take a job as a stenographer. Catherine is a very attractive young woman, and the audience, watching the family dynamic unfold, realizes that Eddie is affected by her in more than an avuncular way.

The family has just received word that Beatrice's cousins, immigrating illegally, have landed and will be arriving to sleep on their floor. Eddie emphasizes the need for secrecy: "You can quicker get back a million dollars that was stole than a word that you gave away." He recalls a neighbor who had "snitched" to the immigration service on an uncle and that family's brutal retribution. Compliance with the letter of the immigration law was seen not only as *not* justice, but as the greatest betrayal.

The cousins, Marco and Rodolpho, arrive. Rodolpho, the younger of the two, is handsome and unmarried. The characters notice Rodolpho's lightness and blondness.

Three months pass, and Eddie's dislike of Rodolpho takes form. Rodolpho sings and Eddie comments that "he's like a chorus girl or sump'n" and compares Rodolpho unfavorably to Marco, who "goes around like a man." While Eddie waits for Catherine and Rodolpho to return from the movies, Beatrice accuses him of jealousy and asks when she can be a wife again.

Eddie goes to see Alfieri, explaining that he thinks Rodolpho is interested in marrying Catherine only to obtain immigration papers and that "[t]he guy ain't right." Alfieri tells Eddie that he needs to let go and that "the law is not interested in this." Alfieri tells the audience that at that moment he could foretell the whole tragedy that would unfold and wondered at his "powerlessness to stop it." He even visited a wise old woman, confiding in her. Her response: "Pray for him."

Law, represented by the lawyer, appears quite helpless as this drama unfolds. Even the resort to female wisdom, a role Portia also played in *The Merchant of Venice*, cannot erase the sense of the law's passivity and lack of responsiveness. Can prayer be the only recourse in human relations, or can the law do more both as an aspirational ideology and as a vehicle to concretely better human life? The division here between the so-called private sphere and the public sphere creates part of the tension in the law's role.

A sequence of gender role exhibitions follows: first the audience sees Rodolpho and Catherine dancing, then Eddie boxing with Rodolpho, saying he'll teach him, and finally Marco lifting a chair with one hand in a show of strength as a sort of warning to Eddie. As Rodolpho's brother, Marco is aware of the rising tension, and strength is the only protection he knows to use. A rule of law theoretically replaced the idea that might makes right, but with this appeal to strength, turning to the law once again appears the choice of a loser.

The gender dynamics continue in a scene where Eddie kisses Catherine on the lips and then kisses Rodolpho on the lips, to show Catherine "what he [Rodolpho] was like." Here again the imputation of homosexuality is considered the most damning thing that can be said about a man. The dominant cultural value of heterosexuality finds no challenger to Eddie's kiss, a reminder of the kiss Judas gave to Jesus, betraying him at the Last Supper.

Catherine is planning to marry Rodolpho. Eddie responds that Marco and Rodolpho must move out. He returns to visit Alfieri, who again tells him that nothing can be done.

As foreshadowed, Eddie places an anonymous call to immigration, which picks up Marco, Rodolpho, and two newly arrived submarines, illegal immigrants who are relatives of others in the neighborhood. Marco spits on Eddie and proclaims, "I accuse that one!"

Alfieri bails Rodolpho out; Rodolpho still plans to marry Catherine. Alfieri explains to Marco that he must promise not to kill Eddie if he wants to be bailed out. Marco considers such a promise dishonorable. He asks what will happen to Eddie. Alfieri replies, "Nothing. If he obeys the law, he lives. That's all." Marco replies, "The law? All the law is not in a book." "Yes," says Alfieri. "In a book. There is no other law."

But to Marco, Eddie is someone who degraded his brother, robbed his children of Marco's income, and mocked his work. "Where is the law for that?" he asks. When Alfieri says, "There is none," Marco shakes his head and says, "I don't understand this country."

On the day of the wedding Marco comes to fight Eddie, who pulls a knife. Marco, who is very strong, bends the knife into Eddie's heart.

Alfieri's closing words are ambiguous:

> Most of the time we settle for half and I like it better. But the truth is holy, and even as I know how wrong he was, and his death useless, I tremble, for I confess that something perversely pure calls to me from his memory—not purely good, but himself purely, for he allowed himself to be wholly known and for that I think I will love him more than all my sensible clients. And yet, it is better to settle for half, it must be! And so I mourn him—I admit it—with a certain . . . alarm.

Eddie had deceived himself. Though he kissed Catherine, he denied he loved her, just as he denied his role in calling immigration. Eddie did not live by the code of honor of his heritage. His call to immigration was a serious violation of that unwritten law. Yet the lawyer, the bridge between the Old World and the New, loved him.

In the world viewed from the bridge, heterosexuality is privileged and strict gender roles are observed. The economic reality of class drives much of the unwritten code of the immigrants. Whiteness remains privileged as the default assumption, but color is made an issue in terms of blondness (Eddie calls Rodolpho "Dane" as a taunt in several places). In the face of these systems of privilege the law is helpless; the lawyer can only watch as the story unfolds.

For Arthur Miller, a Jewish playwright, the theme of assimilation into a dominant culture and the role of law must have touched close to his heart. He chose not to use Jewish characters as a setting for this theme. And when he tried to imagine the kind of conflict that could cause a relatively new American to violate the code of ethics of his culture, he turned to heterosexual romantic love as a great motivator of human behavior.

Eddie paid with his life for violating the code of his ancestors. Why would the law, represented by Alfieri, love him? No character celebrates his reporting to immigration; following that rule of law does not render him heroic. Alfieri's affection for Eddie seems to stem from Eddie's helplessness in the face of love, suggesting a male bonding privilege between Alfieri and Eddie. Even the view of law from the bridge has a male tilt to it; the bridge is a man. For law truly to bridge people's many different worlds, it needs consciously to seek a more inclusive voice.

C. Fires in the Mirror

Anna Deavere Smith's documentary theater on race and anti-Semitism, set in the modern United States, reveals again a preoccupation with justice and injustice. The issue of race, which has not often been present in mainstream theater,[25] comes to center stage in this dialogue about justice.

Fires in the Mirror[26] represents a new kind of theater. The intersections between the characters as part of the fabric of society is made visible in the person of Smith; she plays all the characters and conveys multiple viewpoints and diverse perspectives. These different viewpoints are missing in the courtroom drama of the adversary system, which needs advocates for the missing voices: the *Bakke* case, for example, was litigated without representation of those most seriously affected by it—the beneficiaries of affirmative action.

The theater piece is a perfect vehicle to give voice to the unrepresented. The desire for justice resonates through the words of her characters, which convey the depth of our cultural aspiration for justice. Yet her work reveals the very different ways people envision justice. What is justice when one group's aspirations for justice might exist only at the expense of another group? Yet surely justice must be more than a zero sum game. There must be enough justice to go around.

Fires in the Mirror is dedicated to the residents of Crown Heights, Brooklyn, and to the memory of Gavin Cato and Yankel Rosenbaum, who both died there. The Crown Heights conflict began on August 19, 1991, when a car that was part of a procession carrying the Lubavitcher Hasidic spiritual leader ran a red light and landed on the sidewalk.

The car hit and killed Gavin Cato, who was seven years old, Black, and from Guyana, and seriously injured his cousin Angela. Word on the street was that a private Jewish ambulance had helped the driver and his passengers, while the children lay bleeding. Later reports suggested that this statement was untrue, but one must pause to consider the reality of white privilege and devaluation of Black life that could enable many people to believe that rumor.

Members of the Crown Heights Black community reacted with violence against the police and their Lubavitcher neighbors. That evening, a group of young Black men fatally stabbed Yankel Rosenbaum, a twenty-nine-year old Hasidic scholar from Australia. Three days of street fighting in the community followed.

The background information published with the play explains that this conflict reflected long-standing tensions in Crown Heights between Lubavitchers and Blacks, "as well as the pain, oppression, and discrimination these groups have historically experienced outside their own communities." Many people have said that white racism, including Jewish racism, and Black anti-Semitism played a role in the events that unfolded, including the media reporting of those events. Again the isms language masked the systemic privileging of whiteness and Christianity as part of the dominant cultural vision that enabled both of these groups to be labeled "other" by society and by each other.

Like the passive viewer standing on the bridge, law remains a bystander, not intervening as these people are construed as other, as not part of the societal mainstream. In fact, law plays a role in their continued exclusion. The police intervention in the Black community was experienced by them as an invasion. The failure to take steps to punish the traffic violation and vehicular homicide made law seem ineffective. The failure to prosecute and convict someone for Rosenbaum's murder similarly made law seem irrelevant.

The people of Crown Heights all want justice from an unresponsive system. The rule of law seems irrelevant to their lives. They are situated outside the hierarchy created by the rule of law. In contrast, the characters in *The Merchant of Venice* play out their emotions in the courtroom, the universe of the rule of law. Portia, Bassanio, and Antonio hold privileged places in the hierarchy, where they can speak to the duke.

Law has failed to address the conflicts in the Crown Heights community. A child is dead. A rule of law that fails to address his death seems meaningless. Nor can revenge be justice. A rule of law was theoretically created to contain the kind of human passion that reaches for that avenue of response. But it is failing in the modern era, even as we still aspire to justice. Rodney King asked, "Can't we all just get along?" In *Fires in the Mirror*, Anna Deavere Smith as one individual playing all these characters shows we are one community. She shows us the voices of the many, including our different aspirations for justice. But it seems we cannot all get along until privilege is seen; only then can justice be adequately discussed.

Lessons from the Plays

Read together, these three plays show a progression in attitudes about the possibility and desirability of assimilation into the dominant culture. *The Merchant of Venice* represents the dominant cultural lens, including its anti-Semitic perspective, suggesting that assimilation into the dominant culture is the "happy ending."

A View from the Bridge is more ambivalent; even the resolution of the play is subject to interpretation. We as the audience, and ultimately as citizens, must decide what we think about Eddie's following the rule of law to turn in illegal immigrants and his death under the code of rules his culture followed. What does "settling for half" mean in the context of a rule of law and aspiration for justice? We need much more conversation about justice, and we need to examine the systems of privilege that impede the realization of justice.

Anna Deavere Smith uses theater to begin that dialogue. Her characters in *Fires in the Mirror* speak in their own words, as close to their own voice as we in the theater are likely to witness. We can hear and see their different views. Smith stays to talk with the audience after many performances, inviting people from the community where the performance has occurred to join her on stage to engage the issues. This possibility for conversation in a public space happens almost nowhere, because as a culture we go out to be passively entertained at movies or concerts, or stay at home watching television. This is a theater of possibility, with the potential of building community.

The resolution of *The Merchant of Venice*, with its insistence on assimilation, is obsolete. But a nonassimilationist society must allow different views and yet still function with basic rules—whether rules for small group interaction or rules codified as law—that allow us to fulfill our human potential. Rules about respecting people, taking responsibility, and trying not to harm others are basic to human survival. But the dominant culture of democratic liberalism emphasizes the individual over community. We think in terms of individual rights, individual achievement, individual merit, rarely of connection, community, and responsibility.

If assimilation is not the answer that can push us toward rules basic for human survival, then the creation of a public space to discuss the aspiration for justice becomes even more critical. As Cornel West writes in the Foreword to *Fires in the Mirror*, "public performance has a unique capacity to bring us together." This unique character of theater creates a public space where we can talk about real issues facing our society.

As the next chapter explains, the classroom can also be that kind of public space. Access to education becomes a critical vehicle, another avenue of public space where these issues can be addressed.

Chapter 8

Stephanie M. Wildman

Teaching and Learning toward Transformation
The Role of the Classroom in Noticing Privilege

Lani Guinier begins her book about democracy with a story about children at play. She was reading the *Sesame Street Magazine* with her four-year-old son, Nikolas. The magazine pictured four children raising their hands to play tag, and two children voting to play hide-and-seek. As Guinier explains,

> The magazine asked its readers to count the number of children whose hands were raised and then decide what game the children would play. Nikolas quite realistically replied, "They will

An earlier version of this chapter appeared as Stephanie M. Wildman, *Privilege and Liberalism in Legal Education: Teaching and Learning in a Diverse Environment*, 10 BERKELEY WOMEN'S L. J. 88 (1995), copyright © 1995 by Stephanie M. Wildman. Reprinted with permission.

play both. First they will play tag. Then they will play hide-and-
seek." Despite the magazine's "rules," he was right. To children,
it is natural to take turns.[1]

This lesson about inclusion, fundamental to children and to democracy, needs to be relearned in our university classrooms, particularly
law school classrooms. Childhood innocence has an intuitively inclusive view of the world. When we set up categories and boundaries as
part of the thinking and socialization process, that inclusiveness
becomes undermined. True, we must have rules, but why not rules of
inclusion?

It is auspicious that at this historic point so many scholars are talking about matrices, crossroads, intersections, and Koosh balls. These
discussions recognize that sameness and difference, privilege and
subordination, inhere in every individual. But the categories by
which we label characteristics can become barriers that block learning and the links that make learning possible. Categories that carry
more cultural weight than others create the biggest barriers. While
we are all Koosh balls consisting of many threads coming together,
these threads are not all treated the same in our culture. Some of
these categories have meanings that resonate and create subordinating assumptions. Inclusive community will not be created until we
recognize the social significance of these exclusionary categories and
discuss the privileging dynamic they create. Silence is not an acceptable response.

In 1990s America, race is such a category. For example, I have a
friend who is seventeen. She has blond hair, hazel eyes, and pale skin.
She identifies herself as Latina and Black and white, because that is
her racial heritage. She is also smart, and she is a swimmer. She was
excitedly telling a school friend about her acceptance to UC San
Diego, which had awarded her a merit scholarship.

Her so-called friend said to her, "Yeah, but what race did you put?"

The use of that category, race, had the power to erase all her accomplishments, her late nights studying to get good grades, and her efforts at swim practice. The use of race in the conversation made her feel unworthy and somehow "less than." Her friend's highlighting of race, implying here nonwhiteness, made her feel diminished, even though she is proud of her race.

Power categories[2] such as race shape our vision of the world and of ourselves. Most of us with white privilege lead pretty white lives. Consider our schools, shops, medical buildings, neighborhoods. In most places where we spend time, we are in white settings, unless we act affirmatively to seek a racially integrated environment. These white lives make it hard for us to see the privilege that accompanies us in our daily, ordinary existence.

Our universities and the law schools within them are some of the few places where we have a real chance to participate in an integrated community, one that is truly diverse across these many power categories. Institutions need to acknowledge this ongoing project of building a diverse community as part of the work of the institution.[3] It is important to make this work visible, because it is a continuing process. One white law professor I know asked why she should continue working on racism when she had already spent eight hours at an unlearning racism workshop, and no end to racism was in sight.

Power systems that interfere with building community have no quick fix, but building community needs to be our life—all of our lives. A white person can recede into privilege and not worry about racism whenever she or he chooses. People of color cannot. Men and heterosexuals can ignore the system of gender hierarchy, if they choose. Women and gay men cannot.

Recently in my torts class I assigned groups of students to write think pieces on tort reform.[4] Part of my purpose was to create a setting in which the students could discuss the issues with each other. I wanted them to think together about what a more perfect world would look like. The local legal newspaper published the best of these reflections, along with the students' photographs, in a tort reform symposium.

Even in these outwardly benign circumstances, the institutional hierarchies played themselves out. One of the groups whose work was published consisted entirely of women of color. After the piece appeared I said to one of these women, "You must feel good about having your work published."

"Well," she shrugged, "people are saying that our piece was chosen because we've done so badly in law school that you were just trying to help us out. You know, because you're sympathetic to minorities in law school."

I looked at her in disbelief as many thoughts swirled through my head. Although it was unfounded and untrue, this rumor mill reaction, that their papers were somehow *less than*, prevented these students from enjoying the experience of publication in the same way that the white students could. For this Latina student, even her fleeting happiness at seeing her name in print and having her article published was taken away. She was denied even this shred of self-confidence and achievement by the unnamed entity of "they" that defined the community as white and this student as other.

"You can't even enjoy having your work published, like the rest of the students in the symposium," I said to her.

She nodded, "It's just the way it is here. I'm not surprised."

But *I* was surprised that students would act that way toward each other. Part of my white privilege is being able to be surprised, to forget what people of color cannot forget in order to survive in predominantly white institutions. But in addition to surprise, I felt both despair and anger that my teaching effort, trying to help *all* students publish their work, would result in pain to these students of color.

And so it is very important that we, as members of a law school community, take this discussion about power systems and privilege into our classrooms. Classroom dynamics take place, of course, within the context of the systems of power and privilege that this book has been discussing. The culture in which we live spills into our classrooms, infecting them before we even write on the clean chalkboard. And legal education has its own form of intellectual elite privileging, another Koosh ball strand, in the dynamic of the law school classroom.

The traditional Socratic method, the *Paper Chase* model, uses the classroom to insult, to intimidate, to model the professor as one who knows all. Most classrooms are constructed auditorium-style, with an elevated, louder-voiced, single person in the front, and rows of observing, passive students looking up. This passivity and authoritarian focus is the expectation and paradigm of legal education. No wonder Duncan Kennedy calls it training for hierarchy.[5]

I once saw Gloria Watkins, also known as bell hooks, stepping down into such a room and walking among the audience, talking. Her proximity created a closeness and was very effective in dispelling the hierarchical aura of the room. Yet some students feel violated when the professor leaves the podium and comes into "their" domain. The professor is still the holder of the privilege, choosing the nature of the interaction.

The authority privilege of the teacher crosscuts with other privilege systems in fascinating ways, because not all professors enter the classroom with the same package of privileges. Every woman professor to whom I have ever spoken about this subject has agreed that men receive a benefit of the doubt, a little chip of "you belong here," that women do not receive when we enter a classroom.[6]

I discussed this phenomenon of male faculty privilege with a male colleague who was quite upset at the idea. He felt that this privilege notion was a disparagement of male teachers. He worked hard, he said, in the classroom, and if he did not, students would not say he was a good teacher. I agreed with him that students would quickly discount a poor teacher, male or female. But I was talking about the presumption of competence that occurs *before* anyone says a word. That certain skepticism students feel toward me because I am a woman (some have told me so) means that I have to work harder when I stand up in front of a class. And I wear my white privilege when I walk to the podium.

We as teachers struggle with our privilege and position in the hierarchy that is legal education; students struggle too. Silence in the classroom or lack of participation can happen when we make students feel as though they do not belong. While this feeling is something we may create quite unintentionally, sexual subordination has been a stock-in-trade of legal education for several generations, privileging male students who can participate in the laughter at women's expense.

A Yale law student reports this story of a so-called joke told by her evidence professor about a hearsay case in which a man killed his wife during an argument. The wife had called her mother during the fight; the legal issue was whether the mother's statement, reporting what her daughter had said to her over the phone during the fight, was admissible. The professor described the facts and then lightheartedly said, "I guess that's the last argument they'll ever have." The student described her reaction in this internal monologue:

> Shall I raise my hand and tell him that it's not funny to make jokes about battered women? Should I talk with him after class? He's not receptive to questions in class, so maybe I should go up later, but then my peers' attention won't be called to the incident. Meanwhile there is a blank space in my notebook and an evidentiary point lost.[7]

The effect of the gender power system is harmful to our women students. As teachers we have to ensure that everyone is part of the educational process, and this means that we as teachers and students, members of a community, have to think about how our remarks and comments in class are heard. This is basic politeness, not censorship. If we want a community to include all people within it, we will not talk about Kikes when we mean Jewish people or say "chicks" to refer to women. We are being hurtful when we use these words that wound, as Richard Delgado calls them.[8]

Also we need to notice who is talking in our classes and who is not. Notice who the professor is calling on, who is being affirmed, who is given longer chances, who is passed over quickly. When women students in my class are doing 10 percent of the talking and they are in fact 50 percent of the class, I have asked them to stay after class and talk about it. These invisible dynamics need to be named and brought out into the open.

My own teaching style is to hear from other people and to listen. The lecture format and the room arrangement grant me the power, privilege me. I understand that this is the art form, but we need to develop better ways to build classrooms. We need to rearrange furniture. And most important, we need to create better ways to communicate with each other for community building. No one is immune from the difficulty of this process.

The struggle taking place in the academy to make gender, race, and sexual orientation a part of the law school curriculum is part of this difficult struggle toward inclusive community. This movement has been fueled primarily by students and a number of law professors, many of whom are members of the Society of American Law Teachers. These members of the legal academy recognize the relevance and importance of issues relating to race, gender, and sexual orientation, not only to our lives but also to our teaching and learning.

Exciting innovations have come from this effort, including new classes, casebooks, and scholarship on subjects like sex discrimination and the law, critical race theory, and gender roles and the law. An increased acceptance of these issues in some classrooms and institutions has resulted as well.

Unfortunately, the response within the legal academy to this drive to recognize issues of race, gender, and sexual orientation has not been wholly positive. The downside is marked by law professors who race[9] and gender their classroom hypotheticals and final exams with African American criminals, the detailed offensive language of gay and lesbian bashing, or the grisly particulars of domestic violence directed against women. Often, when students complain, the professors answer, "But these things happen. I thought you wanted me to make my class relevant. What do you want anyway?" or something along those lines.[10] We seek more than mere inclusion of race, gender, and sexual orientation in the law school curriculum. We seek understanding as well.

I had a recent "aha experience"[11] about how to discuss this understanding. I was involved in a teaching exercise that crossed several first-year subject areas, including torts, property, contracts, civil procedure, and criminal law. In the problem, an African American family was racially harassed by a white neighbor over a period of months. The harassment included shots fired at the family's home. The police were called to the home numerous times. Both neighbors were tenants of the same landlady, who was white. In the problem, the landlady evicted both tenants, saying that even though the white family was primarily at fault, she did not want to become involved.

One group of students, coming to discuss the problem with other faculty members, explained that they did not believe the landlady had done anything wrong. They could see that the white tenants were culpable. The students even described them as racist. But the students refused to label the landlady racist.

What was the landlady? By calling her "not racist," the students placed her actions beyond reproach in their own imaginations.

Perhaps the students, who were all white, imagined that they might have done the same thing, and they certainly did not believe that they were racists. They simply believed that it was wrong that the African American family had been harassed because of race.

As a group, white people in this culture are very eager to label prejudiced behavior racist and to separate ourselves from that behavior. Society is certainly full of extreme cases of racism. White people are so eager to distance ourselves from racism and spend so much time trying to demonstrate that we are not racist, that we fail to see the systemic privileging of whiteness. This privileging ensures that extreme acts of racism, as well as the daily microaggressions,[12] will continue to exist.

I discussed the student response to the exercise with a colleague. She suggested that white students needed to have an experiential moment, identifying with the African American family, to enable them to understand the harm inherent in racial harassment and in the landlady's complicity. Maybe if they could write down the word or pejorative phrase that would most offend the core of their being and affect their sense of identity, then they could relate to the affront of someone remaining "neutral" about racial harassment and intimidation. My colleague suggested that I have them write down the word and then plug it into the facts of the problem, having them intimidated by a neighbor with those words, and see how they would react to the landlady then evicting them.

Okay, I thought, good idea. I discussed this plan with a second colleague, also involved in teaching the exercise, who said he was not sure that white, male, heterosexual students would have anything to say about what would affect their core identity.

I then asked, "What about 'cheater' or 'wimp'? Religious aspersions? Surely there would be something?" I realized as I spoke that I was confronting the analogy problem about which Trina Grillo and I have written. Although there are limits to the use of analogies between oppressions, the problem remains that analogies may be our only tool to achieve empathy with and understanding about different forms of oppression.[13]

This second colleague replied that he was afraid that for some white male students the most offensive thing one could do would be to call them gay. The problem with using the analogy method to teach about racial oppression is that the comparison does not work. Racial oppression is unique. Comparing oppressions may lead to a false sense of understanding. The lesson about subordination would come at the expense of implicitly validating oppression on the basis of sexual orientation.

This was my own "aha experience," because I found myself trapped, not for the first time, in legal liberalism. Legal liberalism teaches us that all people should be treated equally, fairly, and the same. It is the solid underpinning of the notion of the color-blind Constitution that Clarence Thomas recently advocated.[14] It appeared when John F. Kennedy intoned, with great emotional force, "Race shall play no part in American society."[15] This is our ideal, and it is attractive.

The reality is that if we say race plays no part, then the invisible system of white privilege will inevitably continue. In this status quo of white privilege, the African American family who suffered harassment may now be without a place to live, while the evicted white family finds a new home easily.[16] Even if the African American tenants find a new home, they may be racially harassed and suffer eviction again. The system of white privilege means that the white family is not at risk in the same way.

We must also strive to see the privileging of heterosexuality. There is no real risk to the heterosexual student who is called gay. He does not face job discrimination or have to hide the identity of his family in order to be accepted by his classmates.

Legal liberalism suggests that all individuals are similarly situated in society, absent disadvantaging, unfair treatment. Systemic privilege is not part of legal liberalism's vocabulary. Seeing the privilege of whiteness or heterosexuality takes effort for those privileged; privilege is our norm.

As I mentioned in chapter 2, legal education needs to understand what Frances Ansley called the "power line,"[17] a horizontal line she had drawn on the board at a conference presentation. Ansley asked the audience to consider our location as to race, gender, sexual orientation, and other categories with respect to this line. Those above the line are privileged with respect to those below it. No one contested the reality of privilege and subordination that such a line represented.

For me, the question is how to bring this knowledge about systems of privilege into the classroom and make it live for students. Teaching and learning in a diverse environment require awareness and honesty about systems of privilege. That conversation is hard to achieve where years of education have ignored the existence of these systems.

During a recent orientation week, I tried an exercise that Patricia Cain has done. In this exercise, students choose two or three words to identify themselves, words with deep meaning about who they are and that really articulate their self-image.[18] I had separated the students into smaller groups for another purpose, and I asked them to tell a designated group scribe the words that each student selected. The scribes wrote the words down, without associating them with any particular student. The scribes then read the list of words back to the large group, and so we knew all the words the students had chosen.

Perhaps not surprisingly, given that this was an orientation class on the first day of law school, the words the students chose to describe the essence of their identity were terms like "afraid," "unprepared," and "intimidated." "Cherry Garcia junkie" was the most descriptive choice. The words were mostly superficial, and the students were very protective about their beings.

Cain's experience, having done this exercise in her seminar class, early on in the semester, was that people of color tended to use words that identified themselves as such whereas, of course, white people *never* used "white" to describe themselves. Similarly, women usually used a gendered word to describe themselves. Had I done this exercise, my own word would probably have been "mother." The only gendered word in the torts orientation class was "feminist." One brave soul did say that. There were no words identifying students' sexual orientation, which is not surprising for gay men and lesbians who might not be out. Those who were out obviously did not feel safe to choose that identification in class at that time.

In spite of the fact that the exercise did not turn out the way it had when Cain did it, I did not regard it as a failure. I used the exercise as an opportunity to talk about what Cain had done and what her results had been, and to comment on the difference between our results and hers. I spoke about the way our world is raced and gendered and how assumptions are made about sexual orientation. The class was very quiet as I said this. I worried that I might have silenced the class forever from open discussion. Since no one stayed after class to talk to me, I really had no way to know.

Fortunately, as the class proceeded, it seemed fine, and all students participated. Since I got the positive feedback I often get from students, I do not think I destroyed the classroom environment. On that first day of class, I raised the idea that these issues, which are usually regarded as taboo in the classroom, could be discussed. That they are taboo was demonstrated by the response; nobody other than the one brave feminist felt that she could make reference to these ideas. My hope was that the door to discussing these issues had been opened at least a little.

Race, gender, and sexual orientation are in the room whether we make them explicit or not, but everyone pretends that they are not noticing. Part of my point here was to say, "let us notice"; it is important both to notice and discuss these subjects with respect, realizing that people situated differently in relation to the power line have very disparate experiences of daily reality. For example, walking into a bank to cash a check may be a racial experience for people of color who face requests for extra identification and even curious stares, while their white counterparts do not. These different experiences of daily reality must be acknowledged in classroom discussions.

A context of institutional support is an important backdrop for such discussions. Part of the reason I felt I could initiate this conversation was because of how good I felt about the law school where I was visiting. I had been attending the orientation classes with the students and listening to what other people told them about the institution's values and culture. The dean said he supported the academic success program.[19] In some institutions the administration does not even pay lip service to this idea. Leaders who want to change the status quo of privilege make a difference.

There are some things I did not say to the class, which upon reflection I wish I had. First of all, regarding race, we live in a world that is raced. We wish it were not so. We have a great mythology about all people being equal. Equality is our aspiration, the goal in our culture, but the fact is that our world does not treat people of all races and ethnicities alike. Our dilemma is how to move from a world where we know the reality is non-equal treatment to the world of our aspirations.

I am afraid one of the main steps American culture has taken toward the goal of equality is to pretend that the aspiration has been achieved. The result is that race becomes a taboo subject in mixed racial groups, or at least a subject that is taboo to talk about in certain ways. For example, in my experience, it is very unusual to find white people standing around and talking about whiteness. We have not given white people the vocabulary to talk about whiteness. We need to begin to develop this political discourse.[20]

The world, of course, is also gendered, and this raises many different issues. No one is going to dispute that there are men and there are women. Probably a lot of people will not even dispute that there is unequal treatment of women and men. There is a growing body of literature acknowledging that women and men have different viewpoints. In torts we now teach about reasonable men and reasonable women.

Presumptions are made about sexual orientation; most often the presumption is that any given individual is heterosexual. We know that is not always true. Even though students in the classroom rarely identify themselves as gay or lesbian, we know that a significant percentage of the students are gay or lesbian. What can we do to create a community where students of all sexual orientations feel comfortable in the classroom? We want *all* students to feel safe and able to talk about these issues and participate in the class as themselves.

Adrienne Davis tells a story, which is fictional but rings true, in which a law professor calls on an African American woman, asking her to comment on the subject as an African American. The story addresses the teacher's power to name the student as African American and to ignore her gender.[21]

Davis and I discussed whether it would have been preferable for the professor to ask if any African American students wanted to answer, thereby giving them the opportunity to identify with the term themselves. We agreed that this approach was still not acceptable. It put African American students on the spot, asking them to take center stage and show off their African American knowledge as if they were in class only to enlighten the white students. This kind of attention comes at great cost to them.

A better pedagogic tactic would be to bring scholars of color into the classroom by referring to their work. There is a growing body of literature written by colleagues of color. Professors and students should be reading this literature and validating it in the classroom. If we bring the views of scholars of color into the classroom, then students of color can express their views in critique or support without being forced to put themselves in the position of educating whites.

We, as teachers on the dominant side of the power line relating to race, gender, or sexual orientation, risk exhibiting our own ignorance. However, it is preferable for us to shoulder this risk rather than further burdening students on the subordinated side of the line. It still costs them when we exhibit our ignorance, but at least students of color should not be forced to the center of attention when it happens.

My own students' comments about making gender, race, and sexual orientation a part of the curriculum were illuminating. Several women students, who stayed after class one day, said that some white male students were uncomfortable because I raised all these issues. The women were not sure what to do about this. They believed it was a learning experience for the men to participate in a classroom that they did not dominate, or feel like they owned. The women believed the men could learn from experiencing any kind of pain in the classroom, whether from feeling excluded by a remark or not being recognized once. Interestingly, the women students were worried about the male students' reaction to missing some privilege. The women wanted to make the men feel comfortable. Never have male students come to express concern about including women more in class.

While I strive to make all students comfortable in the classroom, I remain especially concerned about students on the subordinated side of the power line. I remain concerned that these students, who have been marginal participants in the legal profession, are gripping the table in pain as the racism, sexism, and homophobia of our world resonates through the classrooms in which they are trying to learn.

Our own work needs to begin by looking at our own privileges, which are so difficult to see. Instead of worrying about how not to be racist or sexist or otherwise prejudiced, let's think about the systems of power and the privilege that keep those prejudices intact. Then try to do something about them. For a first step, try to make a friend with someone across the power line, and try to listen carefully to what is important to your friend.

Stephanie M. Wildman and
Margalynne Armstrong

Concluding Thoughts on Noticing Privilege

It is old news that white Americans inhabit a different reality from people of color, particularly African Americans. Yet the shock of white Americans at the news during the trial of O. J. Simpson that police planted evidence or made racist remarks suggests that old news is still invisible to many white people.

Following the not guilty verdict, the media constructed reactions to the verdict along a racial divide and portrayed the mostly female, African American jury as emotional and incompetent. Implicit in this portrayal was the privileging of white reaction to the verdict as rational, objective, and nonbiased. Once again white racial privilege dominated the scene, yet was not discussed. This kind of invisible preference for white opinion and white viewpoint undermines our national ideal of government based on a democratic, participatory perspective.

The different realities for white and Black Americans will endure as long as white privilege remains invisible. Rather than facing this reality of "two nations," many whites continue to discount the relevance of race. They aspire, as do most people of color, to the ideal of Martin Luther King's dream that children be judged by the content of their character and not the color of their skin. But wishing cannot make it so, and our lived reality continues to be that "race matters," as Cornel West has said. Until we pay attention to *how* race matters, acknowledging white racial privilege and the dynamic of subordination that stems from it, efforts to address other power categories may just perpetuate racial oppression.

Paying attention to the systems of privilege that pervade our lives is difficult because these systems are rendered invisible through linguistic constructs. Our language rarely describes privileging but creates categories of oppressions, diminishing them as separate and separable. Discussion of these systems is made more complex because the systems interconnect within individual people, confounding any attempt at labeling. The systems also reinforce each other, strengthening the privileging dynamic that is part of each individual system.

In the workplace these interrelated systems reinforce the existing workplace assumptions, perpetuating existing employment patterns and supporting the economic status quo. In the area of housing, privilege undermines residential desegregation, thereby guaranteeing that de facto school segregation will continue into the twenty-first century.

The role of the media in perpetuating these systems is powerful. From assumptions about who is an authority to decisions about what stories are newsworthy, the media construct reality. Television shows rarely portray interracial communication or friendship. These constructions are interspersed with advertising that reinforces images of normative interactions as heterosexual, mostly white, and consisting of men as doers, actors, and leaders.

It is imperative that we begin to talk about these systems of privilege, yet the very effort to do so may obscure the system of white privilege, unless we are very careful. Attentive listening to the views of others, different from ourselves, is critical to understanding the operation of these systems in daily life.

These systems of privilege create rules for small group dynamics that govern our daily interactions, relations, and discourse. An unwritten rule makes it unacceptable to talk about race or discrimination in the dominant discourse. Those of us with privilege so earnestly want not to discriminate that we privilege our conduct by failing to examine it critically. Without this examination, the systems of privilege are replicated and the cycle of exclusion continues.

And what of the role of law? The ideology of law contains the aspiration for justice, but law itself has been constructed by society under the same unwritten rules so that privilege is not discussed or noticed. The legal system must provide tools to begin the conversation about privilege, recognizing the operation of dominant cultural norms and protecting those outside its operation. Full democratic participation requires inclusion of all members of society.

The law school is the gateway to the profession. In our teaching and in our classrooms we must set examples for the conversations about privilege that must take place, making the previously ignored visible. W. E. B. Du Bois said, "the problem of the twentieth century is the problem of the color-line." Revealing privilege is the key to erasing this line so that race will not be the problem of the twenty-first century as well.

A plea for friendship, for more sharing and less selfishness, tends to fall unheard or be heard with a shrug in our materialistic, individualistic culture. But the plea must be made as we struggle to understand and explain systemic unfairness.

We take pride in individual achievements and accomplishments without acknowledging the invisible systems of privilege that often have made them possible. It is interesting that there is no vocabulary within our system of white male patriarchy to describe the kind of authorship that has led to this book. When I (Stephanie) suggested to Trina, Adrienne, and Margalynne that we be credited as co-authors, each declined. Yet, as I told them, this book could not exist without the friendship and cooperative work that I have done with each with them. Perhaps this collaborative process can serve as an example of work that we all need to do to make systems of privilege visible. We cannot do this work alone; yet we must individually take responsibility for large parts of our own learning. We need to work both on ourselves and with each other.

What can we with white privilege do? "Just give up the privilege" seems both obvious and impossible. But one small way to give up white privilege is to stop pretending that race does not matter, even though our aspiration continues to be that it should not matter. If we stop pretending that race does not permeate our daily life, our class-rooms, and the affairs of government, perhaps we will start to see the operation of white privilege, and other privileges, more clearly. If antisubordination is our shared societal objective, we need to create room for the conversation about how to achieve that goal. We need everyone to be present and the discussion to take place everywhere: in classrooms, workplaces, and meetings. It is up to those of us with privilege to take our first steps toward dismantling this world of invisible preference and examining the privilege revealed.

Notes

Notes to the Introduction

1. Charles R. Lawrence III, *A Dream: On Discovering the Significance of Fear*, 10 NOVA L. J. 627 (1986), republished in Charles R. Lawrence III, *The Word and the River: Pedagogy as Scholarship as Struggle*, 65 SO. CAL. L. REV. 2231, 2231–36 (1992).
2. *Id.* at 2232.

Notes to Chapter 1

1. STEPHEN HAWKING, A BRIEF HISTORY OF TIME 10 (1988).
2. *Id.* at 11.
3. *Id.*

4. *Id.* at 12.

5. See MARILYN FRYE, THE POLITICS OF REALITY: ESSAYS IN FEMI-NIST THEORY 19–34 (1983) (discussing sex marking, sex announcing, and the necessity to determine gender).

6. Angela Harris and Marge Shultz, *"A(nother) Critique of Pure Reason": Toward Civic Virtue in Legal Education,* 45 STAN. L. REV. 1773, 1796 (1993).

7. Anne Fausto-Sterling, *The Five Sexes: Why Male and Female Are Not Enough,* SCIENCES, Mar./Apr. 1993. (Thanks to Gregg Bryan for calling my attention to this article.) See also Frye, *supra* note 5, at 25.

8. Adrienne Rich, *Compulsory Heterosexuality and Lesbian Existence,* in BLOOD, BREAD, AND POETRY, SELECTED PROSE 1979-1985 (1986).

9. See Stephanie M. Wildman and Becky Wildman-Tobriner, *Sex Roles Iced Popular Team?* S.F. CHRON., Feb. 25, 1994, at A23.

10. Rich, *supra* note 8, at 57 ("Heterosexuality has been both forcibly and subliminally imposed on women").

11. Richard Delgado and Jean Stefancic, *Pornography and Harm to Women: "No Empirical Evidence?"* 53 OHIO ST. L. J. 1037 (1992) (describing this "way things are." Because the norm or reality is perceived as including these benefits, the privileges are not visible.)

12. Lucinda M. Finley, *Breaking Women's Silence in Law: The Dilemma of the Gendered Nature of Legal Reasoning,* 64 NOTRE DAME L. REV. 886 (1989).

13. Leslie Bender, *A Lawyer's Primer on Feminist Theory and Tort,* 38 J. LEGAL EDUC. 1 (1988).

14. Taunya Banks, *Gender Bias in the Classroom,* 38 J. LEGAL EDUC. 137 (1988); and Stephanie M. Wildman, *The Question of Silence: Techniques to Ensure Full Class Participation,* 38 J. LEGAL EDUC. 147 (1988).

15. CATHARINE A. MACKINNON, TOWARD A FEMINIST THEORY OF THE STATE 224 (1989).

16. David Margolick, *At the Bar*, N.Y. TIMES, Dec. 4, 1992, at B20. See Adrienne Davis, Trina Grillo, and Stephanie Wildman, *The Invisibility of Privilege: A Comment*, published *sub nom Privilege's Responsibilities Are Too Often Neglected*, S.F. CHRON., Jan. 8, 1993, at A25 (discussing the interplay of privilege and subordination).

17. MacKinnon, *supra* note 15.

18. Sylvia Law, *Homosexuality and the Social Meaning of Gender*, 1988 WIS. L. REV. 187, 197 (1988); Marc Fajer, *Can Two Real Men Eat Quiche Together? Storytelling, Gender-Role Stereotypes, and Legal Protection for Lesbians and Gay Men*, 46 U. MIAMI L. REV. 511, 617 (1992). Both articles describe heterosexism as a form of gender oppression.

19. Peggy McIntosh, *Unpacking the Invisible Knapsack: White Privilege*, CREATION SPIRITUALITY, Jan./Feb. 1992, at 33. Martha Mahoney has also described aspects of white privilege. Martha Mahoney, *Whiteness and Women, in Practice and Theory: A Reply to Catharine MacKinnon*, 5 YALE J. L. & FEMINISM 217 (1993).

20. The quotations around *meant* evidently evoke the unwritten rules that surround the subject of white privilege.

21. McIntosh, *supra* note 19, at 33.

22. *Id.* at 34.

23. *Id.*

24. Rich, *supra* note 8.

25. Fajer, *supra* note 18, at 514.

26. *Id.* at 515.

27. See, e.g., Michael R. Gordon, *Pentagon Spells Out Rules For Ousting Homosexuals; Rights Groups Vow a Fight*, N.Y. TIMES, Dec. 23, 1993, at A1.

28. Fajer, *supra* note 18, at 515.

29. Kimberlè Crenshaw, *Demarginalizing the Intersection of Race and*

Sex: A Black Feminist Critique of Antidiscrimination Doctrine, Feminist Theory and Antiracist Politics, 1989 U. CHI. LEGAL F. 139, 151. Another important exception, Mari Matsuda, urges those who would fight subordination to "ask the other question," showing the interconnection of all forms of subordination:

> The way I try to understand the interconnection of all forms of subordination is through a method I call "ask the other question." When I see something that looks racist, I ask, "Where is the patriarchy in this?" When I see something that looks sexist, I ask, "Where is the heterosexism in this?"

Mari Matsuda, *Beside My Sister, Facing the Enemy: Legal Theory Out of Coalition*, 43 STAN. L. REV. 1183, 1189 (1991).

30. Adrienne D. Davis, *Toward a Post-Essentialist Methodology or a Call to Counter-categorical Practices* (1994 unpublished manuscript on file with the author). See also Adrienne D. Davis, *Identity Notes One: Playing in the Light*, 45 AM. U. L. REV. (1996 forthcoming).

31. bell hooks, *overcoming white supremacy: a comment*, in TALKING BACK: THINKING FEMINIST, THINKING BLACK 113 (1989).

32. See also Jerome McCristal Culp Jr., *Water Buffalo and Diversity: Naming Names and Reclaiming the Racial Discourse*, 26 CONN. L. REV. 209 (1993) (urging people to name racism as racism).

33. Crenshaw, *supra* note 29.

34. The image of the Koosh ball to describe the individual at the center of many intersections evolved during a working session involving Adrienne Davis, Trina Grillo, and me. I believe that Trina Grillo uttered the words, "It's a Koosh ball." San Francisco, California, March 1992.

35. Joan C. Williams, *Dissolving the Sameness/Difference Debate: A Post-Modern Path beyond Essentialism in Feminist and Critical*

Race Theory, 1991 DUKE L. J. 296, 307. Williams acknowledges work by Angela Harris, Mari Matsuda, Patricia Williams, Martha Minow, and Charles Taylor on this identity theme. *Id.* at n. 47.

36. Thus in 1916 Harold Laski wrote, "Whether we will or no, we are bundles of hyphens. When the central linkages conflict, a choice must be made." Harold Laski, *The Personality of Associations*, 29 HARV. L. REV. 404, 425 (1916).

Notes to Chapter 2

1. At least some men now work in the home, but this fact has not blurred the dichotomy between private and public space. Public space is still the norm of work, and as more women enter that public space, they still carry large burdens of work at home, work that has been described as a "second shift." See Arlie Hochschild, *The Second Shift: Employed Women Are Putting in Another Day of Work at Home*, UTNE READER, Mar./Apr. 1990, at 66.

2. Thus a tantrum at a secretary, because it occurs at a location we call "work," is work, but the same tantrum at home is a tantrum, part of human relations, and probably unacceptable behavior. The tantrum at work may be viewed as a professional necessity, particularly if a male executive has one. Thanks to Trina Grillo for this example.

   Furthermore, even workplace benefits continue to privilege men. "[P]ension laws and practices are designed for the way men traditionally work, with no breaks in employment, building earnings, often at a single company." Special from Newsday, *Pension Gap Widening Between Men and Women*, THE RECORD (Hackensack, N.J.), May 15, 1994 at B03.

3. Expectations of how women should behave at work are negotiated in other spaces. DAPHNE SPAIN, GENDERED SPACES 7 (1992).

4. Spain, *supra* note 3. Space geographers do not always see the interactions of the spaces that they survey. Spain, *supra* note 3, at 11, implies that the point of the legal system is to preserve social order and says the legal system is constructed in the courthouse. But of course the legal system is not just in the courthouse—it is in the workplace as well, in the definitions of acceptable workplace behavior (and it is in many other places as well).

5. Segregation in itself may not indicate a lack of power. The question of who controls and defines the space is also significant. Virginia Woolf wrote many years ago of the need for a room of one's own as a way of having space from which to create words and even power. VIRGINIA WOOLF, A ROOM OF ONE'S OWN (1929).

6. See Jerome McCristal Culp Jr., *Autobiography and Legal Scholarship and Teaching: Finding the Me in the Legal Academy*, 77 VA. L. REV. 539, 546-47 (1991) (discussing how the aspiration for neutrality in law cannot be achieved and the default viewpoint, when neutrality is claimed, is white and male).

7. Geduldig v. Aiello, 417 U.S. 484, 496-97, n. 20 (1974); Gilbert v. General Electric, 429 U.S. 125, 135 (1976) (citing Geduldig v. Aiello, 417 U.S. 484, 496-97, n. 20 [1974]).

8. Noticeably absent in the list of categories is sexual orientation. Recent articles have argued that the system of privilege based on sexual orientation is a form of gender oppression. Sylvia Law, *Homosexuality and the Social Meaning of Gender*, 1988 WIS. L. REV. 187, 197 (1988); Marc Fajer, *Can Two Real Men Eat Quiche Together? Storytelling, Gender-Role Stereotypes, and Legal Protection for Lesbians and Gay Men*, 46 U. MIAMI L. REV. 511, 617 (1992).

9. My colleague Peter Kwan has commented that a British colonial accent, as he describes his own way of speaking English, is not associated with privilege. See also Mari Matsuda, *Voices of*

America: Accent, Antidiscrimination Law, and A Jurisprudence for the Last Reconstruction, 100 YALE L. J. 1329 (1991) (describing how one's own voice never sounds accented and accent is always ascribed to the "other").

10. Conversation with Francie Kendall, in San Francisco, California (Oct. 11, 1994).

11. MACK A. PLAYER, FEDERAL LAW OF EMPLOYMENT DISCRIMINATION 12 (1992).

12. 42 U.S.C. § 2000e-2(a)(1), (2) (emphasis added).

13. McDonnell Douglas Corp. v. Green, 411 U.S. 792 (1972); Wards Cove Packing Co. v. Atonio, 490 U.S. 642, 645 (1989).

14. Griggs v. Duke Power Co., 401 U.S. 424 (1971); Wards Cove Packing Co. v. Atonio, 490 U.S. 642 (1989).

15. Martha S. West, *Gender Bias in Academic Robes: The Law's Failure to Protect Women Faculty*, 67 TEMPLE L. REV. 67, 95 (1994).

16. *Id.* at 95-96.

17. 42 U.S.C. § 2000e-2(a) states in full,

> It shall be an unlawful employment practice for an employer —
> (1) to fail or refuse to hire or to discharge any individual, or otherwise to discriminate against any individual with respect to his [*sic*] compensation, terms, conditions, or privileges of employment, because of such individual's race, color, religion, sex, or national origin; or (2) to limit, segregate, or classify his [*sic*] employees or applicants for employment in any way which would deprive or tend to deprive any individual of employment opportunities or otherwise adversely affect his [*sic*] status as an employee, because of such individual's race, color, religion, sex, or national origin. (Civil Rights Act of 1964, 42 U.S.C. § 2000e-2(a)(1), (2))

18. I first described the comparison mode used in equal protection analysis in a 1984 article. Stephanie M. Wildman, *The*

Legitimation of Sex Discrimination: A Critical Response to Supreme Court Jurisprudence, 63 OR. L. REV. 265, 271 (1984).

19. "In practice, this often means that a female plaintiff must come forward with comparative evidence of a similarly situated man who secured more favorable treatment." Martha Chamallas, *Structuralist and Cultural Domination Theories Meet Title VII: Some Contemporary Influences,* 92 MICH. L. REV. 2370, 2395 (1994).

20. Rabidue v. Osceola Refining Co., 805 F.2d 611, 620 (6th Cir. 1986).

21. The development of case law doctrine concerning hostile environment harassment recognizes this connection. See Jane L. Dolkart, *Hostile Environment Harassment: Equality, Objectivity, and the Shaping of Legal Standards,* 43 EMORY L. J. 151, 177 (1994) (describing sexual harassment as gender subordination).

22. Kimberlè Crenshaw, *Demarginalizing the Intersection of Race and Sex: A Black Feminist Critique of Antidiscrimination Doctrine, Feminist Theory and Antiracist Politics,* 1989 U. CHI. LEGAL F. 139; Paulette M. Caldwell, *A Hair Piece: Perspectives on the Intersection of Race and Gender,* 1991 DUKE L. J. 365, 374; Elvia R. Arriola, *Gendered Inequality: Lesbians, Gays, and Feminist Legal Theory,* 9 BERKELEY WOMEN'S L. J. 103 (1994).

23. See, e.g., Moore v. Hughes Helicopter, Inc., 708 F.2d 475 (9th Cir. 1983) described in Crenshaw, *supra* note 22.

24. 490 U.S. 228 (1989).

25. In the sex discrimination arena, the recognition of sexual harassment as a harm is about recognizing privilege, naming the conduct of the perpetrator as negative, and thereby taking away that privilege. See Harris v. Forklift Systems, Inc., 114 S.Ct. 367 (1993). But male privilege remains in other forms.

26. St. Mary's Honor Center v. Hicks, 113 S. Ct. 2742 (1993).

27. He also alleged a violation of 42 U.S.C. §1981, termination based

on race, and a violation of 42 U.S.C. §1983, demotion and termination based on race. *Id.* at 2746. See also Hicks v. St. Mary's Honor Center, 756 F. Supp. 1244, 1245 (E.D.Mo. 1991).

28. See also Cheryl Harris, *Whiteness as Property*, 106 HARV. L. REV. 1709 (1993); and Barbara J. Flagg, *"Was Blind, But Now I See": White Race Consciousness and the Requirement of Discriminatory Intent*, 91 MICH. L. REV. 953 (1993) concerning the privileging of whiteness.

29. See Hicks v. St. Mary's Honor Center, 756 F. Supp. 1244, 1246 n. 3 (E.D.Mo. 1991).

30. Hicks v. St. Mary's Honor Center, 970 F.2d 487, 489 (8th Cir. 1992).

31. Hicks, 113 S. Ct. at 2748 (quoting Hicks, 756 F. Supp. at 1252).

Notes to Chapter 3

1. "The most salient feature of postwar segregation is the concentration of blacks in central cities and whites in suburbs. . . . By 1970, racial segregation in U.S. urban areas was characterized by a largely black central city surrounded by predominantly white suburbs." DOUGLAS S. MASSEY AND NANCY A. DENTON, AMERICAN APARTHEID: SEGREGATION AND THE MAKING OF THE UNDERCLASS 67 (1993).

2. The term was used in 1968 by the Kerner Commission, which wrote, "This is our basic conclusion: Our Nation is moving towards two societies, one black, one white—separate and unequal." REPORT OF THE NATIONAL ADVISORY COMMISSION ON CIVIL DISORDERS 1 (1968) (hereafter Kerner Commission Report). See also ANDREW HACKER, TWO NATIONS: BLACK AND WHITE, SEPARATE, HOSTILE, UNEQUAL (1992).

3. DAVID RUSK, CITIES WITHOUT SUBURBS 5 (1993).

4. 42 U.S.C. § 3604(b). The full text of the act appears at 42 U.S.C. §§ 3601–14 (1988 & Supp. 1992).

5. See, e.g., Kimberlè Williams Crenshaw, *Race, Reform and Retrenchment: Transformation and Legitimation in Antidiscrimination Law*, 101 HARV. L. REV. 1331, 1378–79 (1988), who explains that "the attainment of formal equality is not the end of the story. Racial hierarchy cannot be cured by the move to facial race-neutrality in the laws that structure the economic, political, and social lives of Black people."

6. DAVID DANTE TROUT, THE THIN RED LINE: HOW THE POOR STILL PAY MORE 19 (CONSUMERS UNION OF U.S., INC., WEST COAST REGIONAL OFFICE, 1993).

7. Tim Schreiner, *Simi Valley, South Central L.A.—Sharp Contrasts*, S.F. CHRON., May 1, 1992, at A14.

8. *Id.* In South Central Los Angeles, 67.7 percent of the housing units are renter-occupied. Trout, *supra* note 6, at 47. Even when able to afford to purchase homes, African Americans are subject to bias in home mortgage lending.

> In 1992, African-Americans in California were 1.75 times more likely to be rejected for mortgage loans than white applicants by Citibank and 1.5 times as likely to be rejected by Bank of America . . . . Across the country, from California to New York, minorities are disproportionately denied mortgage loans. Disparities in mortgage loan rejections and in application rates raise serious questions about minority borrowers' access to credit.

> MICHAEL A. TERHORST, THE AMERICAN DREAM: OPENING THE DOOR TO CREDIT AND ENDING MORTGAGE DISCRIMINATION 2-3 (CONSUMERS UNION OF U.S., INC., WEST COAST REGIONAL OFFICE, 1993).

9. Don DeBenedictis, *Cop's Second Trial in L.A.*, A.B.A. J., July 1992, at 16 (quoting Bernard Segal). These attitudes raise the question:

When suburban cops work in urban jobs, which community is better served by the police, the community that employs them or the communities where the police live? The police perform one aspect of their jobs vigorously, arresting African Americans in numbers that are roughly 100 percent higher than their crime rate. Evan Stark, *The Myth of Black Violence*, USA TODAY MAG., Jan. 1992, at 32, 33. "The National Crime Survey indicates that blacks commit 26.3% of violent crimes, which is roughly twice their percentage in the population. However, they comprise over half of those arrested for violent crimes, four times their percentage in the population." *Id.* Despite this arrest rate, inner-city residents receive notoriously poor police protection and service.

10. Kerner Commission Report, *supra* note 2, at 226.

11. In 1990, 6.6 million workers in the United States could be categorized as "working poor"—people who devoted more than half of the year to working or looking for work and who lived in families with incomes below the official poverty level. Jennifer M. Gardner and Diane E. Herz, *Working and Poor in 1990*, 115 MONTHLY LAB. REV. 20, 20 (1992). Furthermore, even though a person does not have remunerative employment, she may work very hard. The process of maintaining eligibility for benefits and the efforts that go into providing for family needs can be intense and exhausting. See Teresa L. Amott, *Black Women and AFDC: Making Entitlement Out of Necessity*, in WOMEN, THE STATE AND WELFARE 280 (ed. Linda Gordon, 1990). This difficulty is exacerbated for homeless families.

12. John O. Calmore, *Exploring the Significance of Race and Class in Representing the Black Poor*, 61 OR. L. REV. 201, 235 (1982).

13. 402 U.S. 137 (1971). Article 34 of the California Constitution provides in Section 1:

> No low rent housing project shall hereafter be developed, con-
> structed, or acquired in any manner by any state public body
> until, a majority of the qualified electors of the city, town or
> county, as the case may be, in which it is proposed to develop,
> construct or acquire the same, voting upon such issue, approve
> such project by voting in favor thereof at an election to be held
> for that purpose, or at any general or special election.

The provision defines, in telling terms, who the local citizenry
must vote to admit:

> For the purposes of this article only "persons of low income"
> shall mean persons or families who lack the amount of income
> which is necessary (as determined by the state public body
> developing, constructing, or acquiring the housing project) to
> enable them, without financial assistance to live in decent, safe
> and sanitary dwellings without overcrowding.

CAL. CONST. art. 34, § 1.

California voters reaffirmed Article 34 in the 1993 election.
Final Election Returns, L.A. TIMES, Nov. 4, 1993, at B6. The elec-
torate rejected Proposition 168, which sought to rescind the
voter approval requirement for the construction of low-income
housing that relies on public money for at least half its funding.
Id.; also see Greg Lucas, *November Ballot's Forgotten Measures,*
S.F. CHRON., Oct. 25, 1993, at A17.

14. James V. Valtierra, 402 U.S. 137, 143 (1971).
15. *Id.* at 141.
16. Boyd v. Lefrak Org., 509 F.2d 1110 (2d Cir. 1975), *cert. denied,*
    423 U.S. 896 (1975).
17. *Id.* at 1118.
18. *Id.* at 1113.

19. CAL. CIV. CODE §§ 51-52 (1994). The Unruh Act has been held to prohibit all "arbitrary discrimination by a business enterprise." *In re* Cox, 474 P.2d 995 (Cal. 1970) (including forms of discrimination that are not specifically mentioned in the Act). See, e.g., Marina Point, Ltd. v. Wolfson, 640 P.2d 115 (Cal.), *cert. denied*, 459 U.S. 858 (1982) (Unruh Act prohibits discrimination against families with children); O'Connor v. Village Green Owners Ass'n, 662 P.2d 427 (Cal. 1983) (Unruh Act prohibits age restrictions, other than in senior citizen complexes).

20. 805 P.2d 873 (Cal. 1991). In *Harris*, low-income public aid recipients who could afford to pay the rent charged by the defendants were nonetheless denied apartments because their gross income was not equal to or greater than three times the amount of rent. *Id.* at 874. Although the plaintiff could demonstrate that she was paying a greater rate of rent for the premises that she occupied at the time of applying for defendant's apartment and had not defaulted, the landlord did not have to consider her individual characteristics. *Id.* at 874-75.

21. For an examination of discrimination against African Americans in hiring, see MARGERY AUSTIN TURNER ET AL., OPPORTUNITIES DIMINISHED: RACIAL DISCRIMINATION IN HIRING (URBAN INSTITUTE REPORT 91–99, 1991).

22. 451 U.S. 100 (1981).

23. *Id.* at 109.

24. *Id.* at 118.

25. *Id.* at 147.

26. Board of Educ. of Okla. City Pub. Sch. v. Dowell, 498 U.S. 237, 243 (1991).

27. 112 S. Ct. 1430 (1992).

28. *Id.* at 1448 (citations omitted).

29. Loren Miller, *Government's Responsibility for Residential Segregation*, in RACE AND PROPERTY 58, 71–72 (ed. John H. Denton, 1964).

Notes to Chapter 4

1. Nancy S. Ehrenreich, *Pluralist Myths and Powerless Men,* 99 YALE L. J. 1177 (1990) (applying sociopolitical analysis to ideas of reasonableness in sexual harassment); Kathryn Abrahms, *Gender Discrimination and the Transformation of Workplace Norms,* 42 VAND. L. REV. 1183 (1989) (situating sexual harassment within a context of the modern workplace); Wendy Pollack, *Sexual Harassment,* 13 HARV. WOMEN'S L. J. 35 (1990) (discussing how women's actual experiences with sexual harassment suggest the need for revising legal standard); Stephanie M. Wildman, *Rise of the Reasonable Woman: The 9th Circuit Acknowledges That Not All Members of Society Share the Same Reality,* L.A. DAILY J., Mar. 11, 1991, at 6; see also Ellison v. Brady, 924 F.2d 872 (9th Cir. 1991) (holding that allegations of sexual harassment be evaluated by the standard of a reasonable woman).

2. Anita Hill first submitted charges of harassment by Clarence Thomas to the full Senate Judiciary Committee on September 23, 1991. David A. Kaplan, *Anatomy of a Debacle,* NEWSWEEK, Oct. 21, 1991, at 26. However, members of Senator Metzenbaum's Labor Committee staff had initially approached Hill in early September 1991, to inquire about Thomas's character. *Id.*; see also Ronald J. Ostrow, *Doubts Raised on Quality of Thomas Investigation,* L.A. TIMES, Oct. 9, 1991, at A1.

3. Edwin Chen and Paul Houston, *Senate Delays Vote on Thomas to Probe Harassment Charges,* L.A. TIMES, Oct. 9, 1991, at A1; Ostrow, *supra* note 2.

   The pattern of failing to take the charges seriously continued during the hearings. Not all evidentiary sources were explored. Two witnesses, Angela Wright and Rose Jourdain, would have described other incidents of sexual harassment by Thomas. These witnesses never appeared in the televised hearings. Ann

Rockwell and Paul Rockwell, *"Thomas Was Obnoxious": Interview Transcripts Reveal Strong Support for Anita Hill's Charges by Two Key Witnesses the Senate Never Called to Testify*, S.F. BAY GUARDIAN, Nov. 13, 1991, at 25.

4. Although the chronology is disputed, the Associated Press reported that Totenberg first aired the story on October 5, 1991. Associated Press, *Thomas: A New Wrinkle for a Nomination "Virtually Assured,"* Oct. 7, 1991, available in LEXIS, Nexis Library; see also Howard Kurtz, *The Legal Reporter's Full Court Press: NPR's Nina Totenberg and Her Anita Hill Scoop*, WASH. POST, Oct. 10, 1991, at D1. *Newsday* ran the story in the printed press on October 6, 1991, two days before the confirmation vote was scheduled. Timothy M. Phelps, *Ex-Aide Says Thomas Sexually Harassed Her*, NEWSDAY, Oct. 6, 1991, at 7. *Newsweek,* however, reports that Totenberg reported the story on October 6. Kaplan, *supra* note 2, at 26.

5. Phelps, *supra* note 4.

6. So I think it's a cruel thing we're witnessing. It's a harsh thing, a very sad and harsh thing, and Anita Hill will be sucked right into the . . . very thing she wanted to avoid most. She will be injured and destroyed and belittled and hounded and harassed, real harassment, different than the sexual kind.

   Quoted in *Comments by Senators on Thomas Nomination*, N.Y. TIMES, Oct. 10, 1991, at B14. Simpson evidently did not regard sexual harassment as injurious, destructive, or belittling.

7. Judith Weinraub, *Harassment on the Hill: Wanda Baucus Told Her Stories, but the Senators Were Unmoved*, WASH. POST, Oct. 18, 1991, at D1 (quoting Wanda Baucus).

8. See, e.g., Carol M. Tucker, *Distortions in Advertising: The Trivialization of American Women,* 10 SOC. ACTION AND L. 12 (1984). In a recent book of dialogues and interviews, bell hooks

and Cornel West discuss the impact of market forces and increasing consumerism on communities. Much of their insight is of particular relevance to the portrayal of women in the media.

> A market culture will promote and promulgate an addiction to stimulation, it will put forward the view that, in order to be alive, one needs stimulation and he/she who is most alive is the person who is most stimulated. You see bodily stimulation projected through the marketing of sexuality, the marketing of sexual stimulation as the major means by which we construct desire.

bell hooks AND CORNELL WEST, BREAKING BREAD 95-96 (1991).

9. Susan Faludi, the Pulitzer winning journalist, provides excellent insight into this phenomenon in her book *Backlash*. Depictions of women in the media generally are negative and degrading, emphasizing women's status as objects to be instructed in appropriate behavior. SUSAN FALUDI, BACKLASH 75-111 (1991). In discussing commercials, Faludi notes that "in 1987, the American Women in Radio & Television couldn't award its annual prize for ads that feature women positively: it could find no ad that qualified." *Id.* at xxi.

10. John Doggett made this message explicit when he testified before the committee and stated, "'Quite frankly, Anita Hill is not worth that type of risk,' . . . not good-looking enough to throw a career away on." *Talk of the Town*, NEW YORKER, Oct. 28, 1991, at 29, 32 (letter commenting on how "a woman's attractiveness will always be held against her, . . . and a woman's unattractiveness will always be held against her, too").

11. Virginia Lamp Thomas, *Breaking Silence*, PEOPLE, Nov. 11, 1991, at 111.

12. Writing after Thomas's confirmation, Steven Shatz asked the question "Who was lynched?" He suggests that it was Hill who was the victim of the confirmation process. He observed that Thomas certainly did not emerge from this process "hanging from a tree." Steven F. Shatz, *Who Was Lynched?* RECORDER, Oct. 28, 1991, at 8; see also G. M. Bush, *Law Professor Speaks on the Hill Hearings*, S.F. DAILY J., Nov. 19, 1991, at 3 (quoting Kimberlè Crenshaw: "The Democrats' neutral fact-finding position left Anita Hill swinging in the wind").

13. Shatz, *supra* note 12, at 8. The metaphoric use of "lynching" should not be allowed to undermine the brutal, historic reality of lynching.

14. *Id.*

15. Letter from Alice Walker to PEOPLE, Dec. 2, 1991, at 5:

> Black women around the country are sharing a rich chuckle at Virginia Thomas's assertion that she believes 'Anita Hill was probably in love with [her] husband.' The mistress on the plantation used to say the same thing about her female slave every time she turned up pregnant by the master.

16. I firmly insist that the Constitution be interpreted in a color-blind fashion. It is futile to talk of a colorblind society unless this constitutional principle is first established. Hence, I emphasize black self-help, as opposed to racial quotas and other race-conscious legal devices that only further and deepen the original problem.

> *The Supreme Court: Clarence Thomas in His Own Words*, N.Y. TIMES, July 2, 1991, at A14.

After an interview with Thomas, Paul Weyrich wrote, "Mr. Thomas personally disapproves of affirmative-action programs and the use of goals and timetables to remedy employment discrimination, but he insists that he enforced such measures during his tenure at EEOC." Weyrich notes that a number of civil rights advocates working with the EEOC under Thomas disagree. Paul Weyrich, *Clarence Thomas: Here Comes the Judge*, WASH. TIMES, Mar. 1, 1990, at E1.

During a lengthy interview with William Raspberry, Thomas repeatedly expressed doubts about the capacity and appropriateness of the civil rights statutes to remedy discrimination. Clarence Thomas, *Are the Problems of Blacks Too Big for Government to Solve? interview by William Raspberry*, WASH. POST, July 17, 1983, at C3.

17. PATRICIA J. WILLIAMS, THE ALCHEMY OF RACE AND RIGHTS 49 (1991).

18. Williams, *supra* note 17, at 242–43 n. 5.

19. John Denvir, *Politics as Performance Art*, RECORDER, Oct. 28, 1991, at 6 ("The emergence of television as the prime source of political information has created a context in which politics has become a performance art. . . . The president does his work in private, and can pick his own photo opportunities. Because Congress acts publicly, it is at a perpetual disadvantage, under the harsh glare of media scrutiny").

20. *Designing Women, "The Strange Case of Clarence and Anita"* CBS television broadcast, Nov. 4, 1991. Set in Atlanta, it features four white female characters in their thirties and forties who own an interior design company. Susan Faludi refers to the show as one of the more positive television depictions of women in the 1980s. Faludi also notes that the show survived due to its audience popularity despite repeated attempts by its network to "chase them off the set." Faludi, *supra* note 9, at 147–48.

21. Two key characters each wore T-shirts emblazoned with these logos. At one point in the show they stood screen left and screen

right; in the middle was a confused female character, who was trying to make sense out of the whole debate. This character had mixed up Bart Simpson with Alan Simpson and Anita Hill with Anita Bryant, dismissing both Anitas as troublemakers with the same hairdo.

22. Neil A. Lewis, *Bar Association Splits on Fitness of Thomas for the Supreme Court*, N.Y. TIMES, Aug. 28, 1991, at A1. The American Bar Association committee evaluating Thomas's fitness to be a justice found him qualified, although two members found him unqualified. No one found him to be well qualified, the highest possible rating. *Id.*

23. Senator Kassebaum continued:

> When some of my male colleagues have suggested that I know nothing about national defense because I am a woman, I have been offended. In the same vein, I have to assume that many of my male colleagues are offended by the notion that they cannot begin to understand the seriousness of sexual harassment or the anguish of its victims.
>
> On the question before us, some women suggest that I should judge this nomination not as a Senator but as a woman, one of only two women in the Senate. I reject that suggestion.

Nomination of Clarence Thomas, of Georgia, To Be An Associate Justice of the Supreme Court of the United States, 137 Cong. Rec. S14661 (daily ed. Oct. 15, 1991) (statement of Sen. Kassebaum).

24. Compare Wards Cove Packing Co. v. Atonio, 490 U.S. 642, 651, 653-61 (1989) (reinterpreting Griggs v. Duke Power to find heightened requirements constituting prima facie disparate impact case under Title VII) with Griggs v. Duke Power Co., 401 U.S. 424, 431 (1971) (initially articulating standards for prima facie case); Richmond v. J. A. Croson Co., 488 U.S. 469, 498-506

(1989) (awarding of minority business set-asides in subcontracting industry amounted to discrimination under Fourteenth Amendment despite city's finding of and articulated attempt to remedy prior discrimination) with Fullilove v. Klutznick, 448 U.S. 448, 476-78, 482-84 (1980) (rejecting constitutional challenge to minority set-aside of federal monies in subcontracting industry); Webster v. Reprod. Health Servs., 492 U.S. 490, 514-16 (1989) (state may define time at which its interest in fetal life becomes compelling) with Roe v. Wade, 410 U.S. 113, 163-65 (1973) (state's compelling interest in protecting fetal life does not begin until end of the first trimester); Patterson v. McLean Credit Union, 491 U.S. 164, 176-78 (1989) (§ 1981 applies only to initial formation of contract, and employment relationship under contract is not covered) with Runyon v. McCrary, 427 U.S. 160 (1976) (applying § 1981 to making and enforcing of contracts in private, nonsectarian school that discriminated on the basis of race).

Rehnquist wrote, "*Stare decisis* is a cornerstone of our legal system, but it has less power in constitutional cases, where, save for constitutional amendments, this Court is the only body able to make changes." *Webster*, 492 U.S. at 518; see also *Patterson* at 172 (Kennedy expresses same sentiment). At least one reporter believes statements by Rehnquist during oral argument may suggest he would overturn Miranda v. Arizona, 396 U.S. 868 (1969), as well as diminish the separation of church and state. See David G. Savage, *The Rehnquist Court*, L.A. TIMES, Sept. 29, 1991, at 12. For scholarly views on the subject, see, for example, John Denvir, *Justice Rehnquist and Constitutional Interpretation*, 34 HASTINGS L. J. 1011 (1983) (orthodox theory of constitutional interpretation fails to explain Rehnquist's judicial philosophy).

25. Ruth Marcus, *Thomas Refuses to State View on Abortion Issue: Nominee Steadfast amid Senators' Questions*, WASH. POST, Sept.

12, 1991, at A1 ("Clarence Thomas yesterday said he had no opinion on whether the Constitution protects the right to abortion and had not discussed the issue, even in a private setting, in the 18 years since the court decided it").

26. John E. Yang and Sharon LaFraniere, *Bush Picks Thomas for Supreme Court*, WASH. POST, July 2, 1991, at A1 ("President Bush yesterday chose Clarence Thomas, a conservative black federal appeals court judge, to replace Thurgood Marshall on the Supreme Court, saying he is 'the best person at the right time'"); Derrick Bell, *Choice of Thomas Insults Blacks*, NEWSDAY, July 10, 1991, at 85 (It was "typically disingenuous" for Bush to nominate Thomas and call him the best-qualified candidate when "there are at least a half-dozen other black judges whose accomplishments, both on the bench and before becoming federal judges, put those of Thomas to shame").

Notes to Chapter 5

1. bell hooks, *overcoming white supremacy: a comment*, in TALKING BACK: THINKING FEMINIST, THINKING BLACK 112 (1989).
2. *Id.* at 113.
3. Essentialist thinking reduces a complex being to one "essential characteristic." For discussions of essentialism, see ALL THE WOMEN ARE WHITE, ALL THE BLACKS ARE MEN, BUT SOME OF US ARE BRAVE: BLACK WOMEN'S STUDIES (ed. Gloria Hull, Patricia Bell Scott, and Barbara Smith, 1982) (a collection of essays on black women's studies) (hereinafter BUT SOME OF US ARE BRAVE); ELIZABETH SPELMAN, INESSENTIAL WOMAN: PROBLEMS OF EXCLUSION IN FEMINIST THOUGHT (1988); Kimberlè Crenshaw, *Demarginalizing the Intersection of Race and Sex: A Black Feminist Critique of Antidiscrimination Doctrine, Feminist*

Theory and Antiracist Politics, 1989 U. CHI. LEGAL F. 139; Angela Harris, *Race and Essentialism in Feminist Legal Theory*, 42 STAN. L. REV. 581 (1990).

4. Lynne Henderson, *Legality and Empathy*, 85 MICH. L. REV. 1574, 1581 n. 37 (1987).

5. ROBERTO UNGER, KNOWLEDGE AND POLITICS 258 (1975).

6. For an excellent discussion of unconscious racism, see Charles Lawrence, *The Id, the Ego, and Equal Protection: Reckoning with Unconscious Racism*, 39 STAN. L. REV. 317 (1987).

7. Crenshaw, *supra* note 3, at 150–51.

8. Parents of young children who try to have a telephone conversation will easily recognize this phenomenon. At the sound of the parent's voice on the phone, the child materializes from the far reaches of the house to demand attention.

9. Harris, *supra* note 3, at 588.

10. *Id.*

11. Gloria Hull and Barbara Smith, *Introduction: The Politics of Black Women's Studies*, in BUT SOME OF US ARE BRAVE, *supra* note 3, at xx.

12. Harris, *supra* note 3, at 601.

13. Angela Harris writes, "In this society, it is only white people who have the luxury of 'having no color'; only white people have been able to imagine that sexism and racism are separate experiences." *Id.* at 604. Harris describes a meeting of women law professors who were asked to pick out two or three words to describe who they were. Harris reports that none of the white women mentioned race; all the women of color did. *Id.*

14. See FRANCES E. KENDALL, DIVERSITY IN THE CLASSROOM: A MULTICULTURAL APPROACH TO THE EDUCATION OF YOUNG CHILDREN 19–21 (1983) (describing the development of racial awareness and racial attitudes in young children). Although the prevalent view would state that children are "oblivious to differ-

ences in color or culture" (*id.* at 19), children's racial awareness and their positive and negative feelings about race appear by age three or four. *Id.* at 20.

15. Judy Scales-Trent, *Commonalities: On Being Black and White, Different and the Same*, 2 YALE J. L. & FEMINISM 305, 305 (1990).

16. *Id.* at 322–24.

17. Standing to talk about the harm of racism has received attention in legal academic circles recently. Randall Kennedy argues that people of color should not receive particular legitimacy within the academy simply because they are of color. Randall Kennedy, *Racial Critiques of Legal Academia*, 102 HARV. L. REV. 1745 (1989). Kennedy takes issue with the writings of several scholars of color whom he characterizes as proponents of a "racial distinctiveness thesis," which holds that the perspective of a scholar who has experienced racial oppression is different and valuable because of this awareness. *Id.* at 1746.

Replying to Kennedy, Leslie Espinoza argues that it is precisely Kennedy's standing as a person of color that gives special voice and power to his message: "Because Kennedy is black, his article relieves those in power in legal academia of concern about the merits of race-focused critiques of their stewardship, and it does so on the 'objective' basis of scholarly methodology." Leslie Espinoza, *Masks and Other Disguises: Exposing Legal Academia*, 103 HARV. L. REV. 1878 (1990). Espinoza discusses the "hidden barriers" (*id.* at 1879), to participation by people of color in the legal academy; these "[s]ubtle barriers create a cycle of exclusion." *Id.* at 1881. The dominant discourse within the legal academy provides an identity to the privileged group as well as "a form of shared reality in which its own superior position is seen as natural." Richard Delgado, *Storytelling for Oppositionists and Others: A Plea for Narrative*, 87 MICH. L. REV. 2411, 2412 (1989).

18. hooks, *supra* note 1, at 117.

19. *Id.* at 118.

20. Patricia Monture, *Ka-Nin-Geh-Heh-Gah-E-Sa-Nonh-Yah-Gah,* 2 CANADIAN J. WOMEN & L./REVUE JURIDIQUE DE LA FEMININE ET LE DROIT 159, 163 (1986).

21. At a later group discussion, these comments about pain were retold by a white woman who was defending the use of personal experience at the summer camp. A white male participant responded, "The pain of minority people is like television, we can turn it on and off as we want to." *Id.* at 167.

    Monture writes, "Did the man intend to belittle my pain and my life? Did he know how deeply he had clawed into my essence? Did that woman intend to appropriate my pain for her own use, stealing my very existence, as so many other White, well-meaning, middle and upper class feminists have done?" *Id.*

22. At one point the camp participants discussed untenured professors as an oppressed group. During the next day's discussion a woman professor of color shared a dream she had had the previous night, in which there was a pain competition, with comparative pain being measured by large thermometers.

23. It is hard to feel the pain of others, to realize how many horrors have been perpetrated, how many terrible things have happened, and to realize the relative privilege (anyone able to read this chapter is more than relatively privileged) that makes one exempt from some of these horrors.

    Another cancer example illustrates how people must block out the pain that surrounds them in order to survive. The doctors and technologists in the radiation therapy department are all nice, friendly people. No one is unkind. But every day I (Trina) am stunned by how they fail to see or acknowledge the vast amounts of pain around them.

    Not only do they not notice this pain, but they may take active steps to discount it if they do see it. One oncology nurse, speaking to a patient undergoing chemotherapy and experiencing nausea, said, "It's just the same as morning sickness, don't make such a big deal about it." By making the comparison, the nurse is implicitly saying, "What you are experiencing is only what I have experienced, and therefore I do not need to listen to your story."

24. Shirley Chisholm, *Racism and Anti-Feminism,* 1 BLACK SCHOLAR 40 (1970). Chisholm, who describes this country as "both racist and anti-feminist" (*id.* at 40), says, "The harshest discrimination that I have encountered in the political arena is anti-feminism." *Id.* at 43.

25. Bernice Johnson Reagon, *Coalition Politics: Turning the Century,* in HOME GIRLS: A BLACK FEMINIST ANTHOLOGY 356–68 (ed. Barbara Smith, 1983) (emphasizing both the difficulty of building coalitions and their critical importance).

Notes to Chapter 6

1. United States v. Jefferson County Bd. of Educ., 372 F.2d 836, 866 (1966).

2. See Alan Freeman, *Legitimizing Racial Discrimination through Anti-Discrimination Law: A Critical Review of Supreme Court Doctrine,* 62 MINN. L. REV. 1049, 1052-57 (1978) (explaining the perpetrator perspective of antidiscrimination law).

3. Herma Hill Kay, *President's Message—Beyond Diversity: Accepting Differences,* AALS NEWSL., Apr. 1989, at 1, 1.

4. *Id.* at 3.

5. Walter O. Weyrauch, *The "Basic Law" or "Constitution" of a Small Group,* 27 (2) J. SOC. ISSUES 49, 53, 59 (1971) (finding that "rules [of a group] are not to be articulated"), reprinted in LAW, JUSTICE, AND THE INDIVIDUAL IN SOCIETY: PSYCHOLOGICAL AND LEGAL ISSUES, ch. 4, at 41, 43, 46 (June Louin Tapp and Felice J.

Levine eds., 1977). David A. Funk commented on this finding:

> I frequently observe this rule operating at this law school. We do certain things in fact, though we sometimes do not want to admit it. If someone identifies and articulates what we really do, the group may change its actions. Our prior rule of behavior has changed because we cannot face its articulation.

Walter O. Weyrauch, *The Family as a Small Group*, in GROUP DYNAMIC LAW: EXPOSITION AND PRACTICE 178 (David Funk ed. 1988) (comments of Funk).

6. Weyrauch, *Basic Law*, *supra* note 5, at 52.

7. DAVID FUNK, GROUP DYNAMIC LAW: INTEGRATING CONSTITUTIVE CONTRACT INSTITUTIONS 86 (1982). The word "integrating" in the title is used in the sense of "producing an integrated, cohesive group" (*id*. at 115), not in the sense of diversification of the group, which is the concern of this chapter. See also *id*. at 497-502 (discussing group dynamic law relating to educational institutions).

8. NADYA AISENBERG and MONA HARRINGTON, WOMEN OF ACADEME, OUTSIDERS IN THE SACRED GROVE 41 (1988). The authors continue:

> Further in all places and times, there are rules emanating from a variety of sources—some decreed by tradition, others by the governing instruments of particular colleges and universities, still others by union contracts that have replaced the older system of professional norms promulgated as desirable standards by the American Association of University Professors.

The authors go on to describe government policies affecting higher education.

9. I am grateful to Charles Lawrence for first pointing out to me the connection between the mirror and affirmative action.

10. Ursula K. Le Guin, *Feeling the Hot Breath of Civilization*, review of *The Storyteller* by Mario Vargas Llosa, N.Y. TIMES BOOK REVIEW, Oct. 29, 1989, at 11.

11. *Id.*

12. Bakke v. Regents of Univ. of Cal., 18 Cal.3d 34, 66, 553 P.2d 1152, 1174, 132 Cal. Rptr. 680, 702 (1976)(Tobriner, J., dissenting).

13. JOEL DREYFUSS and CHARLES R. LAWRENCE III, THE BAKKE CASE: THE POLITICS OF INEQUALITY 172-202 (1979).

14. Title VI of the Civil Rights Act of 1964, § 601, Pub. L. No. 88–352, 78 Stat. 252 (codified as amended at 42 U.S.C. § 2000d [1982]) provides, "No person in the United States shall, on the ground of race, color, or national origin, be excluded from participation in, be denied the benefits of, or be subjected to discrimination under any program or activity receiving Federal financial assistance."

15. Regents of Univ. of Cal. v. Bakke, 438 U.S. 265 (1978) at 421 (Stevens, J., concurring in part and dissenting in part).

16. 438 U.S. at 349 and 356 (Brennan, White, Marshall, and Blackmun, JJ., concurring in part and dissenting in part).

17. Richard Chused, *The Hiring and Retention of Minorities and Women on American Law School Faculties*, 137 U. PA. L. REV. 537, 539 (1988).

18. See Susan Prager, *Prager Critiques Faculty Hiring Traditions*, STAN. L. J., Apr. 3, 1987, at 2 (reprinted from AALS NEWSL., Nov. 1986).

19. This often repeated myth is not true. UCLA students taking the California bar for the first time in the summer of 1989 passed at a rate of 82.1 percent. Memorandum from Academic Dean Daniel J. Lathrope to the faculty at Hastings College of the Law (Dec. 21, 1989) (citing "General Bar Examination Statistics, ABA Approved Law Schools in California").

20. Johnson v. Transportation Agency, 480 U.S. 616 (1987).

21. This language comes from International Brotherhood of Teamsters v. United States, 431 U.S. 324, 342 n. 23 (1977), in which the Court remarked that a defendant's inability to rebut the inference of discrimination came from the total absence of minorities in linedriver jobs.

22. See *Job Offer to Feminist Scholar May Mark Turn*, N.Y. TIMES, Feb. 24, 1989, at B5 (describing the University of Michigan Law School's tenure offer to Catharine MacKinnon, who had been a visiting professor at many schools, but not offered a permanent position); see also Frances Olsen, *Feminist Theory in Grand Style*, book review, 89 COLUM. L. REV. 1147, 1149 n. 14 (1989) (describing the relationship of hiring decisions and scholarship as follows: "As long as an outstanding legal scholar like MacKinnon was not given a tenured teaching post in the United States, feminist scholarship remained vulnerable within legal academia").

23. Richard Wasserstrom, *Racism, Sexism and Preferential Treatment: An Approach to the Topics*, 24 UCLA L. REV. 581 (1977). But see Lucinda Finley, *Transcending Equality Theory: A Way Out of the Maternity and the Workplace Debate*, 86 COLUM. L. REV. 1118 (1986). Finley criticizes Wasserstrom's idea that race or sex should be as socially insignificant as eye color. Finley states, "I sense that we will have lost something very fundamentally human in such a world of no 'real' difference." *Id.* at 1139.

24. K. C. Cole, *The Psychology of Affirmative Action*, EXPLORATORIUM Q., Spring 1986, at 9, 10 (excerpted from NEWSDAY MAG., July 28, 1985) (quoting Hofstadter, *Default Assumptions*, SCI. AM., Nov. 1982).

25. *Id.*

26. Several anecdotal examples of default assumptions in action illustrate this principle. In a final exam in which I designated an

elementary school teacher character as male, 50 percent of the class referred to the teacher as "she." On a different exam, with a different class, when I designated a basketball coach for a girls' team as female, 40 percent of the students referred to the coach as "he." Under the pressure of exam writing, students responded using their default assumptions.

Recently my son came home from nursery school and said, "Mommy, the rabbi came to Shabbat today and told a story." A rabbi's visit was an unusual event—a first. I replied, "Was he good?" My son looked at me with a puzzled expression and said, "The rabbi was a woman." Default assumptions are powerful. They also show that there exists no we/they dichotomy from which any are exempt.

27. See generally Carrie Menkel-Meadow, *Feminist Legal Theory, Critical Legal Studies, and Legal Education or "The Fem-Crits Go to Law School,"* 38 J. LEGAL EDUC. 61 (1988); see also Deborah Rhode, *Feminist Critical Theories,* 42 STAN. L. REV. 617 (1990) (describing the evolution of feminist critical legal theory).

28. *Bitter Tenure Battle Is Won as Panel Decides to Appoint Swift,* NAT'L L. J., Sept. 18, 1989, at 4; see also *Boalt Hall Update,* NAT'L L. J., Nov. 21, 1988, at 4:

Tenured faculty at the University of California at Berkeley School of Law (Boalt Hall) have voted to recommend tenure for Marjorie M. Shultz, who was denied tenure in 1985. The unusual decision closely follows charges by Boalt faculty member Eleanor Swift that her 1987 tenure denial was due to gender discrimination.

29. See Michael Reisman, *Looking, Staring and Glaring: Microlegal Systems and Public Order,* 12 DEN. J. INT'L L. & POL'Y 165, 165 (1983) (describing the phenomenon of staring at someone in a public place when the target of the glance turns to stare back:

"How the target senses the staring, I cannot say, but he [*sic*] almost always does.")

30. See AUDRE LORDE, *Uses of the Erotic: The Erotic as Power*, in SISTER OUTSIDER 53 (1984) (describing the erotic as a resource within women that has been devalued and vilified in Western society). "As women, we have come to distrust that power which rises from our deepest and nonrational knowledge." *Id.* at 53. "Our erotic knowledge empowers us, becomes a lens through which we scrutinize all aspects of our existence, forcing us to evaluate those aspects honestly in terms of their relative meaning within our lives." *Id.* at 57.

31. Harold J. Berman, *The Use of Law to Guide People to Virtue: A Comparison of Soviet and U.S. Perspectives*, in LAW, JUSTICE, AND THE INDIVIDUAL, *supra* note 5, ch. 8, at 75 (1977).

Notes to Chapter 7

1. Judith Shklar points out that injustice is the subject of fiction and drama. She writes, "Every volume of moral philosophy contains at least one chapter about justice, and many books are devoted entirely to it. But where is injustice? To be sure, sermons, the drama, and fiction deal with little else, but art and philosophy seem to shun injustice. They take it for granted that injustice is simply the absence of justice, and that once we know what is just, we will know all we need to know." JUDITH SHKLAR, THE FACES OF INJUSTICE 15 (1990).

2. Regina Austin cautions against the use of terms like "dominant society" or the "black community" because each is "buffeted by challenges from without and from within" and therefore "in a constant state of flux." Regina Austin, *"The Black Community,"* *Its Lawbreakers, and a Politics of Identification*, 65 SO. CALIF. L.

REV. 1769, 1770 (1992). Yet in spite of tensions relating to bright definitional lines, such entities exist.

3. Margaret Jane Radin, *Reconsidering the Rule of Law*, 69 BOSTON U. L. REV. 781, 781 (1989).

4. "Kill the Queen or kill the law," is how Mordred, the villain of the piece, characterizes the king's choice. ALAN JAY LERNER and FREDERICK LOEWE, CAMELOT (1961).

5. See, e.g., MARK KELMAN, CRITICAL LEGAL STUDIES (1987); JAMES BOYLE, CRITICAL LEGAL STUDIES (1994).

6. E. P. THOMPSON, WHIGS AND HUNTERS: THE ORIGIN OF THE BLACK ACT (1975).

7. *Id.* at 262–63.

8. *Id.* at 266.

9. Morton Horwitz, *The Rule of Law: An Unqualified Human Good?* 86 YALE L. J. 561, 566 (1976).

10. PATRICIA WILLIAMS, THE ALCHEMY OF RACE AND RIGHTS 147 (1991).

11. Lynne Henderson, *Authoritarianism and the Rule of Law*, 66 IND. L. J. 379, 398–99 (1991).

12. *Id.* at 398–99.

13. Henderson distinguishes conservatism, "a sense of caution or respect for tradition" (*id.* at 379) from authoritarianism, which "represents inflexibility and oppression." She describes how U.S. Supreme Court jurisprudence recently has manifested "inflexibility, lack of compassion, and approval of oppression." *Id.* at 380. She comments that there has been an "American political turn to the right in the 1980s, together with the resurgence of active manifestations of racism, anti-semitism and nativism."

14. *Id.* at 382.

15. WALTER COHEN, DRAMA OF A NATION: PUBLIC THEATER IN RENAISSANCE ENGLAND AND SPAIN 19 (1985).

16. Cohen continues, "divergent courses of economic and religious

development in England and Spain begin to explain the differences." *Id.* at 20.

17. There is support for this idea later in the play when Solanio says, "I think he [Antonio] only loves the world for him [Bassanio]." WILLIAM SHAKESPEARE, THE MERCHANT OF VENICE 80 (Signet Classic Edition 1965).

18. *Id.* at 49.

19. *Id.* at 54. See also, *id.* at 56, where Antonio says that the devil can cite scripture, after Shylock has quoted the Bible.

20. For "a pound of man's flesh taken from a man is not so estimable, profitable neither as flesh of muttons, beefs, or goats." *Id.* at 58.

21. A footnote in the Signet edition (*id.* at 78) says that complexion means "temperament (not merely coloring)." But the reviling of coloring is not lessened by the inclusion of other characteristics into the reviled set.

22. *Id.* at 79. Later he adds, "Justice! Find the girl! She hath the stones upon her, and the ducats!" *Id.*

23. *Id.* at 116.

24. ARTHUR MILLER, A VIEW FROM THE BRIDGE (Bantam Edition 1961).

25. Notable exceptions include Pearl Cleage, Athol Fugard, Phillip Gotanda, Lorraine Hansberry, Luis Valdez, and August Wilson, playwrights whose work deserves a wider audience.

26. ANNA DEAVERE SMITH, FIRES IN THE MIRROR (1993).

Notes to Chapter 8

1. LANI GUINIER, THE TYRANNY OF THE MAJORITY: FUNDAMENTAL FAIRNESS IN REPRESENTATIVE DEMOCRACY 2 (1994).

2. "Power categories" is my term. In her work on classification Adrienne Davis calls these categories "hegemonic." Adrienne D. Davis, *Toward a Post-Essentialist Methodology or a Call to*

Counter-Categorical Practice (1994 unpublished manuscript on file with the author).

3. I was impressed to learn, when I delivered an early version of this chapter at St. Thomas University School of Law, that the law school had established a human relations committee, which meant that the school community took this process seriously.

4. Another description of this exercise appears in Stephanie M. Wildman, *Bringing Values and Perspectives Back into the Law School Classroom*, 4 SO. CAL. REV. OF L. AND WOMEN'S STUDIES 89 (1994).

5. Duncan Kennedy, *Legal Education as Training for Hierarchy*, in THE POLITICS OF LAW 40 (ed. David Kairys, 1982).

6. *Black Women Law Professors: Building a Community at the Intersection of Race and Gender, A Symposium*, 6 BERKELEY WOMEN'S L. J. 1 (1990–91).

7. Stephanie M. Wildman, *The Question of Silence: Techniques to Ensure Full Class Participation*, 38 J. LEGAL EDUC. 147, 150 (1988).

8. Richard Delgado, *Words That Wound: A Tort Action for Racial Insults, Epithets, and Name-Calling*, 17 HARV. C.R.-C.L. L. REV. 133 (1982).

9. Kendall Thomas describes the use of "race" as a verb to signify the changing meaning of race over time as it is socially constructed. Kendall Thomas, Comments at Conference on Frontiers of Legal Thought, Duke Law School (Jan. 26, 1990), cited in Charles R. Lawrence III, *If He Hollers Let Him Go: Regulating Racist Speech on Campus*, 1990 DUKE L. J. 431, 443 n. 52.

10. See generally PATRICIA J. WILLIAMS, THE ALCHEMY OF RACE AND RIGHTS (1991). Williams describes this phenomenon in the chapter entitled "Crimes without Passion."

11. Conversation with Professor Laurie Zimet, Director, Academic Success Program, Santa Clara University Law School (October

27, 1994), in which she used the phrase "aha experience" to describe the moment of understanding when the learner comprehends a new idea. See Laurie Zimet, *The Academic Success Program at Santa Clara*, SALT EQUALIZER, Apr. 1994, at 9, 10.

12. Peggy C. Davis, *Law as Microaggression*, 98 YALE L. J. 1559 (1989). The term "microaggression" refers to the subtle daily encounters between African Americans and white persons in which the African American is condescended to, or "put down" by the white offender(s). *Id.* at 1560. The law functions as a microaggression for many African Americans as it reflects and enforces perceptions of racial bias. *Id.* at 1568.

13. See chapter 5.

14. *Justice Thomas Denies He's an 'Uncle Tom,'* S.F. CHRON., Oct. 28, 1994, at A3. But see Neil Gotanda, *A Critique of "Our Constitution Is Color-Blind,"* 44 STAN. L. REV. 1 (1991).

15. EYES ON THE PRIZE (Blackside Productions 1987). *Eyes on the Prize*, and its sequel, *Eyes on the Prize II*, were produced by Henry Hampton and broadcast on public television stations. Both series document the civil rights movement with interviews, film clips, and photographs. Constance L. Hays, *Television: Overcoming Obstacles to a Civil-Rights Chronicle*, N.Y. TIMES, Jan. 14, 1990, at 31.

16. See chapter 3.

17. Frances Ansley, Address to Society of American Law Teachers (SALT) Teachers' Conference, University of Minnesota School of Law (Sept. 22–23, 1994).

18. Patricia A. Cain, *Feminist Jurisprudence: Grounding the Theories*, 4 BERKELEY WOMEN'S L. J. 191, 208 (1988–89).

19. The academic success program assists students with diverse backgrounds to succeed academically. The program employs innovative teaching methods to create a learning environment where difference is acknowledged and validated as part of legal education. See generally the symposium issue on *Academic*

Support Programs: Serious (and Unheralded) Work toward Creating Diversity, SALT EQUALIZER, Apr. 1994, at 8.

20. The discourse concerning whiteness is emerging. See IAN F. HANEY LÓPEZ, WHITE BY LAW: THE LEGAL CONSTRUCTION OF RACE (1995); RUTH FRANKENBERG, THE SOCIAL CONSTRUCTION OF WHITENESS: WHITE WOMEN, RACE MATTERS (1993); Barbara J. Flagg, *"Was Blind, But Now I See": White Race Consciousness and the Requirement of Discriminatory Intent*, 91 MICH. L. REV. 953 (1993); Cheryl Harris, *Whiteness as Property*, 106 HARV. L. REV. 1709 (1993); Martha Mahoney, *Whiteness and Women, In Practice and Theory: A Reply to Catharine MacKinnon*, 5 YALE J. L. & FEMINISM 217 (1993); Peggy McIntosh, *White Privilege and Male Privilege: A Personal Account of Coming to See Correspondences Through Work in Women's Studies* (Wellesley College Center for Research on Women Working Paper no. 189, 1988).

21. A. Davis, *supra* note 2.

Bibliography

Abrahms, Kathryn. *Gender Discrimination and the Transformation of Workplace Norms*. 42 VAND. L. REV. 1183 (1989).

AISENBERG, NADYA, and MONA HARRINGTON. WOMEN OF ACADEME, OUTSIDERS IN THE SACRED GROVE. 1988.

ALL THE WOMEN ARE WHITE, ALL THE BLACKS ARE MEN, BUT SOME OF US ARE BRAVE: BLACK WOMEN'S STUDIES, edited by Gloria Hull, Patricia Bell Scott, and Barbara Smith. 1982.

Amott, Teresa L. *Black Women and AFDC: Making Entitlement Out of Necessity*. In WOMEN, THE STATE AND WELFARE, edited by Linda Gordon. 1990.

Angel, Marina. *Women in Legal Education: What It's Like to Be Part of a Perpetual First Wave or the Case of the Disappearing Women*. 61 TEMP. L. Q. 799 (1988).

Ansley, Frances Lee. *Race and the Core Curriculum in Legal Education.* 79 CAL. L. REV. 1511 (1991).

_____. *Stirring the Ashes: Race, Class and the Future of Civil Rights Scholarship.* 74 CORNELL L. REV. 993 (1989).

Arriola, Elvia R. *Gendered Inequality: Lesbians, Gays, and Feminist Legal Theory.* 9 BERKELEY WOMEN'S L. J. 103 (1994).

Austin, Regina. *"The Black Community," Its Lawbreakers, and a Politics of Identification.* 65 SO. CAL. L. REV. 1769 (1992).

_____. *Sapphire Bound!* 1989 WIS. L. REV. 539.

Banks, Taunya. *Gender Bias in the Classroom.* 38 J. LEGAL EDUC. 137 (1988).

BECKER, MARY, CYNTHIA GRANT BOWMAN, and MORRISON TORREY. FEMINIST JURISPRUDENCE: TAKING WOMEN SERIOUSLY. 1994.

BELL, DERRICK. AND WE ARE NOT SAVED: THE ELUSIVE QUEST FOR RACIAL JUSTICE. 1987.

_____. FACES AT THE BOTTOM OF THE WELL: THE PERMANENCE OF RACISM. 1992.

Bender, Leslie. *A Lawyer's Primer on Feminist Theory and Tort.* 38 J. LEGAL EDUC. 1 (1988).

BENDER, LESLIE, and DAAN BRAVEMAN. POWER, PRIVILEGE AND LAW: A CIVIL RIGHTS READER. 1995.

Black Women Law Professors: Building a Community at the Intersection of Race and Gender, A Symposium. 6 BERKELEY WOMEN'S L. J. 1 (1990–91).

BOYLE, JAMES. CRITICAL LEGAL STUDIES. 1994.

Cain, Patricia A. *Feminist Jurisprudence: Grounding the Theories.* 4 BERKELEY WOMEN'S L. J. 191 (1988-89).

_____. *Teaching Feminist Legal Theory at Texas: Listening to Difference and Exploring Connections.* 38 J. LEGAL EDUC. 165 (1988).

Caldwell, Paulette M. *A Hair Piece: Perspectives on the Intersection of Race and Gender.* 1991 DUKE L. J. 365.

Calmore, John O. *Exploring the Significance of Race and Class in Representing the Black Poor.* 61 OR. L. REV. 201 (1982).

Casebeer, Ken. *The Empty State and Nobody's Market: Class/Power and the Constitutional Economy of Race and Gender.* 1995. Unpublished manuscript.

Chamallas, Martha. *Structuralist and Cultural Domination Theories Meet Title VII: Some Contemporary Influences.* 92 MICH. L. REV. 2370 (1994).

Chang, Robert. *Toward an Asian American Legal Scholarship: Critical Race Theory, Post-Structuralism, and Narrative Space.* 81 CAL. L. REV. 1241 (1993).

Chisholm, Shirley. *Racism and Anti-Feminism.* 1 BLACK SCHOLAR 40 (1970).

Chused, Richard H. *The Hiring and Retention of Minorities and Women on American Law School Faculties.* 137 U. PA. L. REV. 537 (1988).

COHEN, WALTER. DRAMA OF A NATION: PUBLIC THEATER IN RENAISSANCE ENGLAND AND SPAIN. 1985.

Cole, K. C. *The Psychology of Affirmative Action.* EXPLORATORIUM Q., Spring 1986.

Colker, Ruth. *Anti-subordination above All: Sex, Race, and Equal Protection.* 61 N.Y.U. L. REV. 1003 (1986).

Crenshaw, Kimberlè Williams. *Demarginalizing the Intersection of Race and Sex: A Black Feminist Critique of Antidiscrimination Doctrine, Feminist Theory and Antiracist Politics.* U. CHI. LEGAL F. 139 (1989).

————. *Race, Reform and Retrenchment: Transformation and Legitimation in Antidiscrimination Law.* 101 HARV. L. REV. 1331 (1988).

Culp, Jerome McCristal, Jr. *Autobiography and Legal Scholarship and Teaching: Finding the Me in the Legal Academy.* 77 VA. L. REV. 539 (1991).

————. *Water Buffalo and Diversity: Naming Names and*

Reclaiming the Racial Discourse. 26 CONN. L. REV. 209 (1993).

Davis, Adrienne D. *Identity Notes One: Playing in the Light.* 45 AM. U. L. REV. (1996, forthcoming).

_____. *Toward a Post-Essentialist Methodology or a Call to Counter-categorical Practices.* 1994. Unpublished manuscript.

Davis, Adrienne, Trina Grillo, and Stephanie Wildman. *The Invisibility of Privilege: A Comment,* published *sub nom Privilege's Responsibilities Are Too Often Neglected.* S.F. CHRON., Jan. 8, 1993, at A25.

Davis, Peggy C. *Law as Microaggression.* 98 YALE L. J. 1559 (1989).

Delgado, Richard. *Storytelling for Oppositionists and Others: A Plea for Narrative.* 87 MICH. L. REV. 2411 (1989).

_____. *Words That Wound: A Tort Action for Racial Insults, Epithets, and Name-Calling.* 17 HARV. C.R.-C.L. L. REV. 133 (1982).

Delgado, Richard, and Jean Stefancic. *Critical Race Theory: An Annotated Bibliography.* 79 VA. L. REV. 461 (1993).

_____. *Images of the Outsider in American Law and Culture: Can Free Expression Remedy Systemic Social Ills?* 77 CORNELL L. REV. 1258 (1993).

_____. *Pornography and Harm to Women: "No Empirical Evidence?"* 53 OHIO ST. L. J. 1037 (1992).

Denvir, John. *Justice Rehnquist and Constitutional Interpretation.* 34 HASTINGS L. J. 1011 (1983).

_____. *William Shakespeare and the Jurisprudence of Comedy.* 39 STAN. L. REV. 825 (1987).

Dolkart, Jane L. *Hostile Environment Harassment: Equality, Objectivity, and the Shaping of Legal Standards.* 43 EMORY L. J. 151 (1994).

Dominguez, David. *Beyond Zero-Sum Games: Multiculturalism as Enriched Law Training for All Students.* 44 J. LEGAL EDUC. 175 (1994).

Donovan, Dolores, and Stephanie M. Wildman. *Is the Reasonable Man Obsolete? A Critical Perspective on Self-Defense and*

Provocation. 14 LOY. L. A. L. REV. 435 (1981).

DREYFUSS, JOEL, and CHARLES R. LAWRENCE III. THE BAKKE CASE: THE POLITICS OF INEQUALITY. 1979.

Ehrenreich, Nancy S. *Pluralist Myths and Powerless Men.* 99 YALE L. J. 1177 (1990).

Espinoza, Leslie. *Masks and Other Disguises: Exposing Legal Academia.* 103 HARV. L. REV. 1878 (1990).

Fajer, Marc. *Can Two Real Men Eat Quiche Together? Storytelling, Gender-Role Stereotypes, and Legal Protection for Lesbians and Gay Men.* 46 U. MIAMI L. REV. 511 (1992).

FALUDI, SUSAN. BACKLASH. 1991.

Fausto-Sterling, Anne. *The Five Sexes: Why Male and Female Are Not Enough.* SCIENCES, Mar./Apr. 1993.

Finley, Lucinda M. *Breaking Women's Silence in Law: The Dilemma of the Gendered Nature of Legal Reasoning.* 64 NOTRE DAME L. REV. 886 (1989).

_____. *Transcending Equality Theory: A Way Out of the Maternity and the Workplace Debate.* 86 COLUM. L. REV. 1118 (1986).

Flagg, Barbara J. *Enduring Principle: On Race, Process, and Constitutional Law.* 82 CALIF. L. REV. 935 (1994).

_____. *"Was Blind, But Now I See": White Race Consciousness and the Requirement of Discriminatory Intent.* 91 MICH. L. REV. 953 (1993).

FRANKENBERG, RUTH. THE SOCIAL CONSTRUCTION OF WHITENESS: WHITE WOMEN, RACE MATTERS. 1993.

Freeman, Alan. *Legitimizing Racial Discrimination through Anti-Discrimination Law: A Critical Review of Supreme Court Doctrine.* 62 MINN. L. REV. 1049 (1978).

FRYE, MARILYN. THE POLITICS OF REALITY: ESSAYS IN FEMINIST THE-ORY. 1983.

Gardner, Jennifer M., and Diane E. Herz. *Working and Poor in 1990.* 115 MONTHLY LAB. REV. 20 (1992).

Gotanda, Neil. *A Critique of "Our Constitution Is Color-Blind."* 44 STAN. L. REV. 1 (1991).

GUINIER, LANI. THE TYRANNY OF THE MAJORITY: FUNDAMENTAL FAIRNESS IN REPRESENTATIVE DEMOCRACY. 1994.

HACKER, ANDREW. TWO NATIONS: BLACK AND WHITE, SEPARATE, HOSTILE, UNEQUAL. 1992.

HANEY LÓPEZ, IAN. WHITE BY LAW: THE LEGAL CONSTRUCTION OF RACE. 1995.

Harris, Angela. *Race and Essentialism in Feminist Legal Theory.* 42 STAN. L. REV. 581 (1990).

Harris, Angela, and Marge Shultz. *"A(nother) Critique of Pure Reason": Toward Civic Virtue in Legal Education.* 45 STAN. L. REV. 1773 (1993).

Harris, Cheryl. *Whiteness as Property,* 106 HARV. L. REV. 1709 (1993).

Henderson, Lynne. *Authoritarianism and the Rule of Law.* 66 IND. L. J. 379 (1991).

_____. *Legality and Empathy.* 85 MICH. L. REV. 1574 (1987).

Higginbotham, A. Leon. *An Open Letter to Justice Clarence Thomas from a Federal Judicial Colleague.* 140 U. PA. L. REV. 1007 (1992).

Hochschild, Arlie. *The Second Shift: Employed Women Are Putting in Another Day of Work at Home.* UTNE READER, Mar./Apr. 1990.

hooks, bell. *overcoming white supremacy: a comment.* In TALKING BACK: THINKING FEMINIST, THINKING BLACK. 1989.

_____. TEACHING TO TRANSGRESS: EDUCATION AS THE PRACTICE OF FREEDOM. 1994.

hooks, bell, and CORNEL WEST. BREAKING BREAD. 1991.

Horwitz, Morton. *The Rule of Law: An Unqualified Human Good?* 86 YALE L. J. 561 (1976).

Ikemoto, Lisa. *Traces of the Master Narrative in the Story of African American/Korean American Conflict: How We Constructed "Los Angeles."* 66 SO. CAL. L. REV. 1581 (1993).

Jordan, Emma Coleman. *Race, Gender, and Social Class in the*

Thomas Sexual Harassment Hearings: The Hidden Fault Lines in Political Discourse. 15 HARV. WOMEN'S L. J. 1 (1992).

Kay, Herma Hill. *Equality and Difference: The Case of Pregnancy.* 1 BERKELEY WOMEN'S L. J. 1 (1985).

————. *Models of Equality.* 1985 U. ILL. L. REV. 39.

————. SEX-BASED DISCRIMINATION. 3d ed. 1988.

KELMAN, MARK. CRITICAL LEGAL STUDIES. 1987.

KENDALL, FRANCES E. DIVERSITY IN THE CLASSROOM: NEW APPROACH-ES TO THE EDUCATION OF YOUNG CHILDREN. 2d ed. 1996.

Kennedy, Randall. *Racial Critiques of Legal Academia.* 102 HARV. L. REV. 1745 (1989).

Kline, Marlee. *Race, Racism and Feminist Theory.* 12 HARV. WOMEN'S L. J. 115 (1989).

Laski, Harold. *The Personality of Associations.* 29 HARV. L. REV. 404 (1916).

LAW, JUSTICE, AND THE INDIVIDUAL IN SOCIETY: PSYCHOLOGICAL AND LEGAL ISSUES, edited by June Louin Tapp and Felice J. Levine. 1977.

Law, Sylvia. *Homosexuality and the Social Meaning of Gender.* 1988 WIS. L. REV. 187.

————. *Rethinking Sex and the Constitution.* 132 U. PA. L. REV. 955 (1984).

Lawrence, Charles R., III. *The Id, the Ego, and Equal Protection: Reckoning with Unconscious Racism.* 39 STAN. L. REV. 317 (1987).

————. *A Dream: On Discovering the Significance of Fear.* 10 NOVA L. REV. 627 (1986).

————. *The Word and the River: Pedagogy as Scholarship as Struggle.* 65 SO. CAL. L. REV. 2231 (1992).

Littleton, Christine. *Equality and Feminist Legal Theory.* 48 U. PITT. L. REV. 1043 (1987).

————. *Feminist Jurisprudence: The Difference Method Makes.* 41 STAN. L. REV. 751 (1989).

Lopez, Antoinette Sedillo. *On Privilege.* 2 Am. U. J. of Gender and Law 217 (1994).

LORDE, AUDRE. SISTER OUTSIDER. 1984.

MACKINNON, CATHARINE. FEMINISM UNMODIFIED: DISCOURSES ON LIFE AND LAW. 1987.

_____. TOWARD A FEMINIST THEORY OF THE STATE. 1989.

Mahoney, Martha R. *Segregation, Whiteness, and Transformation.* 143 U. PA. L. REV. 1659 (1995).

_____. *Whiteness and Women, in Practice and Theory: A Reply to Catherine MacKinnon.* 5 YALE J. L. & FEMINISM. 217 (1993).

_____. *White Working Men, Law, and Politics: Transformation and the Social Construction of Race.* 1995. Unpublished manuscript.

Margolick, David. *At the Bar.* N.Y. TIMES, Dec. 4, 1992, at B20.

MASSEY, DOUGLAS S., and NANCY A. DENTON. AMERICAN APARTHEID: SEGREGATION AND THE MAKING OF THE UNDERCLASS. 1993.

Matsuda, Mari J. *Affirmative Action and Legal Knowledge: Planting Seeds in Plowed-Up Ground.* 11 HARV. WOMEN'S L. J. 12 (1988).

_____. *Beside My Sister, Facing the Enemy: Legal Theory Out of Coalition.* 43 STAN. L. REV. 1183 (1991).

_____. *Looking to the Bottom: Critical Legal Studies and Reparations.* 22 HARV. C.R.-C.L. L. REV. 401 (1987).

_____. *Public Response to Racist Speech.* 87 MICH. L. REV. 2320 (1989).

_____. *Voices of America: Accent, Antidiscrimination Law and a Jurisprudence for the Last Reconstruction.* 100 YALE L. J. 1329 (1991).

_____. *When the First Quail Calls: Multiple Consciousness as Jurisprudential Method.* 11 WOMEN'S RIGHTS LAW RPTR. 7 (1989).

MATSUDA, MARI, CHARLES R. LAWRENCE, RICHARD DELGADO, and KIMBERLÈ CRENSHAW. WORDS THAT WOUND: CRITICAL RACE THEORY, ASSAULTIVE SPEECH, AND THE FIRST AMENDMENT. 1993.

McIntosh, Peggy. *Unpacking the Invisible Knapsack: White Privilege.* CREATION SPIRITUALITY, Jan./Feb. 1992, at 33.

Menkel-Meadow, Carrie. *Feminist Legal Theory, Critical Legal Studies, and Legal Education or "The Fem-Crits Go to Law School."* 38 J. LEGAL EDUC. 61 (1988).

MILLER, ARTHUR. A VIEW FROM THE BRIDGE. Bantam Edition. 1961.

Miller, Loren. *Government's Responsibility for Residential Segregation.* In RACE AND PROPERTY, edited by John H. Denton. 1964.

Minow, Martha. *Foreword: Justice Engendered.* 101 HARV. L. REV. 10 (1987).

_____. MAKING ALL THE DIFFERENCE: INCLUSION, EXCLUSION, AND AMERICAN LAW. 1990.

Monture, Patricia A. *Ka-Nin-Geh-Heh-Gah-E-Sa-Nonh-Yah-Gah.* 2 CANADIAN J. WOMEN & L. 159 (1986).

Olsen, Frances. *From False Paternalism to False Equality: Judicial Assaults on Feminist Community, Illinois 1869-1895.* 84 MICH. L. REV. 1518 (1986).

OMI, MICHAEL, and HOWARD WINANT. RACIAL FORMATION IN THE UNITED STATES: FROM THE 1960S TO THE 1980S. 1986. 2d ed., 1994.

Oppenheimer, David Benjamin. *Distinguishing Five Models of Affirmative Action.* 4 BERKELEY WOMEN'S L. J. 42 (1988).

_____. *Negligent Discrimination.* 141 U. PA. L. REV. 899 (1993).

Peller, Gary. *Race Consciousness.* 1990 DUKE L. J. 758.

PLAYER, MACK A. FEDERAL LAW OF EMPLOYMENT DISCRIMINATION. 1992.

THE POLITICS OF LAW: A PROGRESSIVE CRITIQUE, edited by David Kairys. 1982. Rev. ed., 1991.

Pollack, Wendy. *Sexual Harassment.* 13 HARV. WOMEN'S L. J. 35 (1990).

RAC-ING JUSTICE, EN-GENDERING POWER: ESSAYS ON ANITA HILL, CLARENCE THOMAS, AND THE CONSTRUCTION OF SOCIAL REALITY, edited by Toni Morrison. 1992.

Radin, Margaret Jane. *Reconsidering the Rule of Law.* 69 BOSTON U. L. REV. 781 (1989).

Reagon, Bernice Johnson. *Coalition Politics: Turning the Century.* In HOME GIRLS: A BLACK FEMINIST ANTHOLOGY, edited by Barbara Smith. 1983.

Reich, Charles. *Law and Consciousness.* 10 CARDOZO L. REV. 77 (1988).
_____. OPPOSING THE SYSTEM. 1995.

Reisman, Michael. *Looking, Staring and Glaring: Microlegal Systems and Public Order.* 12 DEN. J. INT'L L. & POL'Y 165 (1983).

Rhode, Deborah. *Feminist Critical Theories.* 42 STAN. L. REV. 617 (1990).
_____. JUSTICE AND GENDER: SEX DISCRIMINATION AND THE LAW. 1989.

Rich, Adrienne. *Compulsory Heterosexuality and Lesbian Existence.* In BLOOD, BREAD, AND POETRY, SELECTED PROSE 1979-1985. 1986.

ROSALDO, RENATO. CULTURE AND TRUTH: THE REMAKING OF SOCIAL ANALYSIS. 1989.

RUSK, DAVID. CITIES WITHOUT SUBURBS. 1993.

Scales-Trent, Judy. *Commonalities: On Being Black and White, Different and the Same.* 2 YALE J. L. & FEMINISM 305 (1990).
_____. NOTES OF A WHITE BLACK WOMAN: RACE, COLOR, COMMUNITY. 1995.

SHAKESPEARE, WILLIAM. THE MERCHANT OF VENICE. Signet Classic Edition, 1965.

SHKLAR, JUDITH. THE FACES OF INJUSTICE. 1990.

SMITH, ANNA DEAVERE. FIRES IN THE MIRROR. 1993.

SPAIN, DAPHNE. GENDERED SPACES. 1992.

SPELMAN, ELIZABETH. INESSENTIAL WOMAN: PROBLEMS OF EXCLUSION IN FEMINIST THOUGHT. 1988.

THOMPSON, E. P. WHIGS AND HUNTERS: THE ORIGIN OF THE BLACK ACT. 1975.

Tucker, Carol M. *Distortions in Advertising: The Trivialization of*

American Women. 10 SOC. ACTION & L. 12 (1984).

UNGER, ROBERTO. KNOWLEDGE AND POLITICS. 1975.

Wasserstrom, Richard. *Racism, Sexism and Preferential Treatment: An Approach to the Topics.* 24 UCLA L. REV. 581 (1977).

Weiss, Catherine, and Louise Melling. *The Legal Education of Twenty Women.* 40 STAN L. REV. 1299 (1988).

WEST, CORNEL. RACE MATTERS. 1993.

West, Martha S. *Gender Bias in Academic Robes: The Law's Failure to Protect Women Faculty.* 67 TEMPLE L. REV. 67 (1994).

Weyrauch, Walter O. *The "Basic Law" or "Constitution" of a Small Group.* 27 (2) J. SOC. ISSUES 49 (1971).

_____. *The Family as a Small Group.* In GROUP DYNAMIC LAW: EXPOSITION AND PRACTICE, edited by David Funk. 1988.

Wildman, Stephanie M. *Bringing Values and Perspectives Back into the Law School Classroom.* 4 SO. CAL. REV. OF L. AND WOMEN'S STUD-IES 89 (1994).

_____. *The Legitimation of Sex Discrimination: A Critical Response to Supreme Court Jurisprudence.* 63 OR. L. REV. 265 (1984).

_____. *The Question of Silence: Techniques to Ensure Full Class Participation.* 38 J. LEGAL EDUC. 147 (1988).

Wildman, Stephanie M., and Becky Wildman-Tobriner. *Sex Roles Iced Popular Team?* S.F. CHRON., Feb. 25, 1994, at A23.

Williams, Joan C. *Dissolving the Sameness/Difference Debate: A Post-Modern Path Beyond Essentialism in Feminist and Critical Race Theory.* 1991 DUKE L. J. 296.

WILLIAMS, PATRICIA J. THE ALCHEMY OF RACE AND RIGHTS. 1991.

Williams, Wendy. *Equality's Riddle: Pregnancy and the Equal Treatment/Special Treatment Debate.* 13 N.Y.U. REV. L. & SOC. CHANGE 325 (1985).

Index

128, 136, 141–42, 168, 174
absence of mention in Title
  VII law, 34
See also gay; heterosexism,
  heterosexist; homophobia;
  privilege; race; sexual orientation; sexual preference
liberalism, 159, 170–71

MacKinnon, Catharine, 15, 123,
  208
McIntosh, Peggy, 17–18
majoritarian culture
  See dominant culture
"Make a friend," 3–4, 176
Mason, Perry, 67–68
Matsuda, Mari, 184, 185
melting pot message, 113
  See also affirmative action
Merchant of Venice, The, 142,
  147–51, 153, 157, 158, 159
merit
  See affirmative action
micro–aggression, 135, 169, 214
microlegal system
  See exclusion, cycle of
Miller, Arthur, 142, 151–2, 155
Miller, Judge Loren, 64
minority
  See African American; Asian
  American; Black; Latino,
  Latina; privilege; race

Minow, Martha, 185
multiculturalism, 103
  See also affirmative action;
  diversity; integration

pain sweepstakes, 98, 204
  See also analogy, analogies
Paper Chase, The, 127, 165
  See also Socratic method
pedagogy
  See teaching techniques
personal power, 132–34, 135
  and erotic knowledge, 210
physical ability, xi
  See also physically challenged;
  privilege
physically challenged, 89, 95
  See also physical ability; privilege
Portia, 147–50, 153, 157
Powell, Justice Lewis, 114–16, 121
power line, 29, 171, 173, 175
Price Waterhouse v. Hopkins,
  38–39
privilege, 41
  and the able–bodied, 95
  analysis, advantages of, 5
  and language, xi, 9–13
  and the media, 67–84, 178
  and the role of law, 62
  and societal norms, 29
  choosing whether to struggle
    against oppression, 16–17, 163